One
To
Remember

The 1982 North Carolina Tar Heels NCAA Championship Team, Then and Now

David Daly

Photographs by Hugh Morton

Introduction by John Kilgo

Publishers's Cataloging in Publication
(Prepared by Quality Books Inc.)

Daly, David. R.
   One to remember: the 1982 North Carolina Tar
Heels NCAA Championship Team, then and now /
David Daly; photography by Hugh Morton; introduction
by John Kilgo.
   p. ill. cm.
   ISBN 1-878086-10-3

   1. University of North Carolina–Basketball–Biography.
I. Morton, Hugh. II. Title: One to Remember: The 1982
North Carolina Tar Heels NCAA Championship Team,
then and now.

GV884.A1C3   796.323
                               QBI91-1386

Printed in the United States of America

Cover Design: Harry Blair
Book Design: Elizabeth House
Production Assistance: Cherie Cummings

Down Home Press
P.O. Box 4126
Asheboro, N.C. 27204

To all who are part of the "Carolina Family."
You contributed to Carolina's success, and you, too, are champions.

To Kathi and my family.

To "Chi Chi." We miss you.

The 1982 NCAA Basketball Championship trophy.

1981-82 NORTH CAROLINA BASKETBALL TEAM

Front row (l-r): Trainer Marc Davis, Assistant Coach Roy Williams, Head Coach Dean Smith, Jim Braddock, Jeb Barlow, Chris Brust, Lynwood Robinson, Co-Head Manager Chuck Duckett, Assistant Coach Eddie Fogler, Assistant Coach Bill Guthridge. Back row (l-r): Manager David Hart, Manager Ralph Meekins, Dean Shaffer, Michael Jordan, James Worthy, John Brownlee, Timo Makkonen, Warren Martin, Sam Perkins, Matt Doherty, Cecil Exum, Buzz Peterson, Co-Head Manager David Daly. (Note: Dean Shaffer left the team before the NCAA tournament for personal reasons). *Photo courtesy of UNC Sports Information Department.*

Contents

Introduction

This book about the 1981-82 North Carolina basketball team is the story of a championship.

Even more than that, it's a story about people, their love and loyalties; a story about togetherness, toughness, unselfishness and a lot of pride.

This was Dean Smith's 21st North Carolina team, the seventh he had taken to the NCAA Final Four. While that record was envied by coaches all over the United States, there were some sportswriters and broadcasters who, because UNC had not won a national championship under Smith, alleged that he "couldn't win the big game."

That was pure nonsense and it needed to be buried. This team, the 1981-82 Tar Heels, dug the hole, buried the allegation, and brought the NCAA title back to Chapel Hill.

• • •

You have to understand that Dean Smith doesn't talk in terms of wins and championships. He has always believed in building a team from the first day of pre-season practice on October 15th. You have to take care of the fundamentals, the little things, to be playing your best basketball in March, and Smith always prepared that way.

This team, though, was on a mission from the time practice started. It began a year before, when the Tar Heels surprised the entire nation by advancing to the NCAA championship game before losing to Indiana in Philadelphia. UNC was in charge of that game and playing well until sophomore star James Worthy was whistled for three first-half fouls. Indiana, with Isiah Thomas and other stars, won the game in the second half.

So, when practice began in October, 1981, Carolina had added new players, including a precocious kid from Laney High in Wilmington, N.C., by the name of Michael Jordan, and had a true team leader in senior point guard Jimmy Black.

On the very first day of practice that year, as the team huddled before leaving the court for the showers, they chanted: "One, two, three, 30."

Six months later, after a night of celebration in New Orleans, Jordan explained that chant this way: "This team wanted to be happy on the morning of the 30th of the third month of the year."

Just so happens that would be the morning after the NCAA championship game.

This team developed a special chemistry from the first game of the season. It was not a team of much depth, but this was before the shot clock, when games could be "shortened" by delaying tactics.

The starting lineup was sophomore Matt Doherty and junior James Worthy at forward, sophomore Sam Perkins at center, freshman Michael Jordan at big guard and senior Jimmy Black at point. Junior Jim Braddock played in relief of Black, and senior Chris Brust got a little time off the bench in the frontcourt. Also, freshman Buzz Peterson, a guard from Asheville, N.C., came along late in the season to earn some playing time.

Adding to the pressure the team would face along the way, it was picked No. 1 before the season began. But that was the national picture. The national situation can always take care of itself later. The neighborhood fights would have to be settled first, and in the Atlantic Coast Conference, that usually meant North Carolina and some other team would have at it. This year, that "some-other-team" would be Virginia, which featured 7-foot-3 All-America center Ralph Sampson.

Carolina started the season with style. It beat excellent teams, including Kentucky, Southern Cal, Rutgers and Kansas in the early going. After a 75-39 bombing of South Florida, USF coach Lee Rose, who had taken teams from UNC-Charlotte and Purdue to the Final Four, said: "They came at us like a blue tidal wave. It was like living a nightmare."

Carolina was 10-0, ranked No. 1 in the nation, when No. 2 Virginia came to Carmichael Auditorium for the first big showdown of the season. It was a classic struggle. Neither team would back away. The Cavaliers led 32-28 at halftime, but Carolina's defense turned the tide in the second half. The Tar Heels prevailed 65-60 with balanced scoring as Sampson responded with 30 points, half of Virginia's total.

1

That game was played on January 9th, and after the game Virginia players spoke of Carolina having to come to Charlottesville on February 3rd for a rematch.

The Tar Heels were 13-0 when Wake Forest came to Carmichael on January 21st. Perkins took ill with a virus at the pregame meal and didn't dress for the game. Carolina never got in sync all night as the Deacons won in an upset, 55-48. Worthy had 20 points for Carolina, but Jordan hit only three of 11 field goal attempts.

Carolina won its next three and went to Charlottesville 16-1. With a capacity crowd in University Hall absolutely rocking the place, the game was rarely a contest. Virginia did everything right. The Cavaliers hit an amazing 31 of 49 from the field. Sampson had 18 points and 12 rebounds. The final score was Virginia 74, UNC 58.

This was more than a loss; it was an embarrassment. Black called a team meeting, at the end of which he said, simply: "We're not going to lose another game."

The Tar Heels went on a tear, and won eight in a row heading into the ACC Tournament in Greensboro, including a 69-51 pasting of Wake Forest on the road.

Carolina's first two ACC Tournament games were routine. The Tar Heels beat Georgia Tech 55-39, then N.C. State 58-46. Both teams had tried to slow down play against favored Carolina.

Then came the championship game on Sunday afternoon, a game on national televison, between Carolina and Virginia for the ACC bragging rights. This wasn't for the national championship, but the feelings on both sides were as high as if it were.

Both teams had a stirring first half, as Carolina led 34-31. But in the second half, Virginia decided to go into a zone defense, a wise move that played to their strength and negated Carolina's quickness. Trouble was, Carolina had the ball and a two-point lead. UNC coach Dean Smith told his team to back it out, force Virginia out of the zone. Virginia, for some reason, refused to respond. It stayed in the zone. Carolina continued to hold the ball, and when the clock started to tick away, the Cavaliers suddenly learned they had not even committed enough fouls to put Carolina on the foul line. Carolina won the game, 47-45, and this was the catalyst for the shot clock in college basketball. UNC had won the ACC championship and the top seed in the NCAA East.

It was off to Charlotte for a first-round game against James Madison.

Smith has this theory about tournament play: if the favored team survives a major scare in the opening game, it relieves the pressure and the team goes on to play well for the remainder of the tournament.

Well, Carolina certainly survived a huge threat in the first game. James Madison, holding the ball in a spread court, was in position to win until James Worthy, who finished with 15 points, saved Carolina in the last two minutes to lead UNC to a 52-50 victory.

Then it was off to Raleigh for the East Regionals. Carolina's first game was against Alabama, one of the nation's most athletic teams. Only a superb performance by Carolina would do. Alabama was indeed that good. But the Tar Heels were superb and advanced with a 74-69 win.

Next up was Villanova, which featured stars John Pinone, Ed Pinckney and point guard Stewart Granger, one of the best in the country. Carolina didn't mess around against the Villanova zone. The Tar Heels led 28-22 at halftime, opened up some breathing room in the second half en route to a 70-60 win and a second straight trip to the Final Four.

If anyone ever doubted what this team was about, the doubt was cleared up after the team from Chapel Hill won the NCAA East. As the rest of the team cut the nets down in Reynolds Coliseum, James Worthy said: "These aren't the nets I want."

Those nets were in the New Orleans Superdome, site of the Final Four.

Carolina was on its way.

• • •

The Final Four had four powerful teams. Carolina's first opponent on Saturday afternoon was Houston, a team that had beaten Missouri in St. Louis to reach the Final Four. Recognize these names? Clyde Drexler, Akeem Olajuwon, Lyndon Rose, Michael Young and Larry Micheaux? Houston, under coach Guy Lewis, was loaded.

The other semifinal game had Georgetown, seeded No. 1 in the West, against Louisville.

North Carolina broke the gate with fury against the Cougars. When Worthy passed to Perkins for a baseline jumper with 15:12 left in the first half, the Tar Heels led 14-0.

"Houston is an excellent team," Smith said, "and we knew they would come back."

Houston never led, but trailed only 59-55 with 2:53 left in the game. Carolina held on to win, 68-63.

"We're delighted to be in the Final Two," Smith said. "Houston is a very underrated team. Drexler and

Olajuwon are going to be great pros."

Louisville didn't have the guns to stop Georgetown, and the Hoyas won that game to make it Carolina-Georgetown for the national championship. Georgetown coach John Thompson and Dean Smith were close friends then, still are today.

Without question, these teams that would play for the national championship in the Superdome that Monday night were the two best teams in the nation.

• • •

Carolina's team traditionally huddled before it took the court for pre-game warmups. The walk from the dressing room to the Superdome court was a long one, and the Tar Heels stacked their hands together and stayed that way for what seemed an inordinately long time.

"We told each other in the huddle that we had accomplished every goal up to that moment," Jimmy Black said, "and we had only one left. That would take 40 minutes of our best basketball, and we were determined to play our best game."

Georgetown had a fiercely talented team, led in the backcourt by senior guard Sleepy Floyd, who came from James Worthy's hometown of Gastonia. But the real force for the Hoyas was Patrick Ewing, a 7-foot freshman with strength, quickness, and great athletic ability.

This was everything a championship battle should be. North Carolina's biggest lead in the first half was three points, Georgetown's best was a 12-6 advantage. The Hoyas led at halftime, 32-31, and the 61,612 fans in attendance were treated to a real basketball clinic between two tough and competitive teams.

There were big plays all game long. Understand, with no shot clock and in a game between two evenly matched and well-coached teams, a two-point lead with the basketball seemed huge in the second half. The teams traded baskets and one-point leads through the first eight minutes of the half.

Then, Georgetown was set to make a run. The Hoyas led 49-45 and had the ball. Carolina freshman Buzz Peterson intercepted a pass at midcourt and passed it to Worthy, who not only slammed the ball home, but was fouled by Floyd on the play. Worthy made the free throw, and the Tar Heels were only one point behind.

The next crucial play came in a pass that you've probably seen many times since. Down 53-50, UNC's Matt Doherty hit Worthy with a beautiful touch pass for another dunk.

Face it, this game was going to the wire, to the last second.

Remember this one? Jordan drives left of the lane, Ewing comes over to block the shot, and Jordan shoots the ball high off the glass with his left hand for a 61-58 UNC lead with 3:26 left.

Ewing then hit a basket where the ball danced all around the rim before falling, and then after a missed UNC foul shot, Floyd hit from the lane, another shot that bounced two or three times before falling through.

That gave Georgetown the lead at 62-61 with 57 seconds left.

Carolina took a timeout with 32 seconds left. Smith told his team that Georgetown would likely stay in a zone defense and pay special attention to an attempted lob to Worthy or Perkins. That should open an area on the left wing for Michael Jordan.

"We want you to take the shot if it's open," Smith told his prized rookie.

Smith was right. Georgetown was in a zone, paying close attention to Worthy and Perkins. Doherty set up just beyond the foul line, Black on the right wing. Black passed to Doherty, who faked a pass inside, drawing the Hoya defense closer to the basket.

Doherty fed Black, who threw over the zone to Jordan. The rookie didn't hesitate. He nailed the shot from about 19 feet.

"I must tell you that I didn't see it go in, though," Jordan confessed later, "because after I shot the ball, I closed my eyes."

Georgetown rushed down the court for the final shot, still with plenty of time. As the Hoyas went into their offense, Fred Brown, with seven seconds left, tossed the ball to a startled Worthy, who dribbled toward the left corner of his own forecourt. Eric Smith fouled Worthy with two seconds left. For some reason, Georgetown took its final timeout before the foul shots.

Worthy missed both shots, but with no timeouts left, Ewing rebounded, passed to Floyd, who let fly from midcourt with Jordan standing too close for comfort. The ball came up short, and the Tar Heels celebrated the national championship.

A couple of things to remember about this team. One, it was one of the few teams Smith has ever taken to the NCAA Tournament that was injury-free. Second, this team was a perfect fit.

Worthy was the acknowledged star, and all he did against Georgetown was hit 13 of 17 from the field in scoring 28 points. Perkins gave Carolina a good defensive player inside, and he also could score. Doherty just

3

wanted to win. He was a passer, a screener, a defensive player, and he could score if you ignored his presence on the court. Jordan was special, even as a freshman. He played fearlessly, and had the competitive heart of a lion. And the spiritual leader was Black, who made it a cause to win this national championship for his coach.

It was an especially touching moment after the championship game, as Smith and Black embraced.

"We got it," Black said, ecstatically.

"I love you," said Smith.

• • •

On the 10-year anniversary of that great Carolina team, fans wonder if it was UNC's best. You'd have a hard time settling that argument.

Remember, the 1977 team, without injuries, probably would have waltzed to the national championship. Three future first-round NBA draft choices all were injured in the NCAA playoffs that year – Phil Ford (elbow), Walter Davis (broken finger on shooting hand), and Tommy LaGarde (knee). Still, that crowd beat Purdue, Notre Dame on St. Patrick's Day, a great Kentucky team when Ford had to miss the second half, and Nevada-Las Vegas, before losing in the championship game to Al McGuire's final Marquette team.

The best ever? Somebody had better at least mention the 1957 Carolina team that went 32-0 and beat Kansas and Wilt Chamberlain in three overtimes for the national championship.

And how about 1984? Had Kenny Smith, the freshman point guard starter, not broken his wrist against LSU in Chapel Hill, this could have been the best. This team killed good teams before the Smith injury. That injury to Smith occurred on January 29th and Carolina was 17-0.

Smith came back in the ACC Tournament, wearing a cast on his injured wrist. But the team was never quite the same. Still, that team went 14-0 in the ACC, 28-3 overall, and featured, among others, Jordan, Perkins, Doherty, Brad Daugherty, Smith, Steve Hale, Buzz Peterson, Joe Wolf and Dave Popson.

Some could also make a good argument for the 1987 team that finished 14-0 in the ACC, 32-4 overall.

• • •

The 1982 Tar Heels, though, don't come in second to any team. They did everything they had to do. After losing that big game at Virginia, they closed with 16 straight wins.

There was a major celebration on Chapel Hill's Franklin Street moments after Carolina's championship was secure. And the next day, when the team arrived home on a warm, sunny day, 25,000 fans filled one side of Kenan Stadium to cheer their heroes.

"It shows that nice guys can finish first," Chancellor Chris Fordham said.

Everybody connected with the team was at that celebration.

Except the coach. Dean Smith, who hates to draw even a flicker of attention away from his players, opted to go home and take his young daughter, Kristen, for a walk.

Matt Doherty put it in perspective when he said: "This championship is a memory that no one will ever be able to take away from us. Years from now when they talk about Carolina basketball, they will talk about this team as if it just played yesterday."

Yes, that's true.

This is the story of that championship. A story that endures 10 years after.

This was Carolina Basketball at its very best. ■

– John Kilgo

4

Foreword

March 29, 1982. Smith. Thompson. Worthy. Ewing. The Final Four. 61,612 fans. Carolina. Georgetown. New Orleans. Chapel Hill. Tar Heels. Hoyas. 17 seconds. Jordan. Champions.

Ten years ago, they were freshmen, sophomores, juniors and seniors. Coaches, trainers and managers. Two established superstars. One rising phenomenon. Role players. North Carolinians and New Yorkers. A Texan, a Tennessean, a Virginian. Even a tall skinny kid from Finland. They were all different, yet united by a goal: to win the NCAA national championship.

These days the memory of the realization of that goal and the historic night in New Orleans is still fresh in the minds of the 1982 Tar Heels.

They were winners.

It had been 25 years since Carolina had won the 1957 NCAA national championship in basketball.

Now it has been 10 years since the 1982 championship.

The decade has passed quickly for that team. They all have gone their separate ways. Some have found success in business, sports or other fields.

Winners.

What did they learn? Where have they been? Where are they going?

Carolina basketball prepares its players for life. That's Dean Smith's goal. Mix learning with work, work with play. If done properly, success is the result. Throw in a little luck, and champions are created.

And what the champions do with their championship is up to them.

This is their story.

Businessmen. Athletes. Teachers. Journalists. Coaches. Lawyers.

Arkansas. South Carolina. Florida. California. Illinois. Texas. Australia. North Carolina.

Chapel Hill.

Home.

Ten years later.... ■

The Starting Five

Jimmy Black
Matt Doherty
Michael Jordan
Sam Perkins
James Worthy

Jimmy Black

"We were all thrown there for a reason. They sprinkled some magic dust over us, and they said this is what's going to happen that year. It was destiny."

Hometown: Bronx, N.Y.
Height: 6-3
Weight: 162
Class: Senior

Under senior Jimmy Black's skillful guidance, the 1982 team was a close-knit group, both on and off the court. Senior leadership is earned, not given, on a Carolina basketball team, and Jimmy worked hard to accomplish that.

"I think that I had paid my dues," he explains. "I learned from some of the older guys how to be a leader. When it was my turn, I just felt like I had the respect of the other people on the team, and we could talk about everything. There wasn't anything hidden from

---

JIMMY'S TEAMMATES give him much of the credit for leading them to the 1982 championship. He shut down better-known guards: Ennis Whatley of Alabama, Stewart Granger of Villanova, Rob Williams of Houston. Yet it was Worthy, Perkins, and Jordan who got the press.

---

anybody. We all felt comfortable. That made it easy.

"I guess everything came together for me as well as the team. We were all a year older. We had been to the Final Four the year before. I didn't like that feeling of losing. If we got back, I didn't want to come away with that same feeling, because I felt awful after that."

Some changes were in order to replace those awful memories of '81.

"I think when you have a bad experience, you try

to do everything different," says Black.

The nets were not cut down after tournament victories in 1981. The feeling of the team was to wait and cut them down at the championship game in Philadelphia. But as a senior leader in 1982, Jimmy disagreed.

"Why shouldn't we?" he says. "We just accomplished something, and I think we should celebrate by cutting the nets down and enjoying it. To do things different and enjoy it a little better was a lot more rewarding for all of us.

"Staying in town (New Orleans, as opposed to staying outside of Philadelphia in '81), getting a chance to see Bourbon Street, cutting the nets down. We wanted to do that, why not enjoy it?"

And enjoy it he did. Jimmy says he knew the day before the championship game that Carolina was going to beat Georgetown. At the private practice held in the Superdome that Sunday afternoon, something strange happened, something uncharacteristic of a Carolina team. A fight almost broke out between two players. "It was ultra intense," Jimmy remembers of that practice session. "Jeb (Barlow) and James (Worthy) were getting ready to get in a fight. I think we had gone about 20 minutes, and I remember Coach (Smith) calling practice off.

"I just knew at that point we were going to win the game, because practice was so intense that we →

8

were wasting our time. Everybody was so focused. We wouldn't have gotten anything accomplished by practicing. All we needed was the game to start. I think that was probably one of the most rewarding things that I felt. I never expressed that to anyone, but I knew at that point that we were going to win that basketball game. I went home with peace of mind."

Jimmy has carried that peace of mind with him through the years. He smiles when he thinks back to those days of glory. He remembers as he knelt down and covered his face at the end of the championship game.

"That's when all the emotions I had hidden for a year finally just broke me down to the point that I just couldn't handle it anymore. I just wanted to let all that emotion out, to regroup, because there was a little bit of time left in the game," he says, laughing. "I just wanted to get it all out and then get myself together so we could go back out and finish the game."

• • •

Now Jimmy speaks of his fond college experience as if it were yesterday. Great. Wonderful. Nice. These are words that come out of his mouth as he looks back.

Leader. Confident. Unselfish. These are words that are spoken by friends, teammates, and fans, when Jimmy's name is mentioned.

"If I can just do my part to help us win, then that was important to me," he says. "I didn't do anything flashy. I didn't do anything that would make you say, 'Man, he's a great player.' But I thought I would do a lot of things to help win games. Instead of sprinting faster, I would run longer."

Jimmy's teammates give him much of the credit for leading them to the 1982 championship. He shut down better-known guards: Ennis Whatley of Alabama, Stewart Granger of Villanova, Rob Williams of Houston. Yet it was Worthy, Perkins, and Jordan who got the press.

Teammate Matt Doherty says, "He was probably one of the most underrated point guards ever to play basketball. It's a hell of a statement, but he didn't get the credit he deserved. You give Jimmy the ball, and you just had to run up court. You knew it was going to get up court. You give Jimmy any defensive assignment, and he's going to lock the guy up, like the guy at Houston (Williams). He didn't score a field goal. Nobody talks about that. Jimmy was a great player, a great leader, and a lot of fun to be around."

After ending his college athletic career on a high

Jimmy Black and Coach Dean Smith discuss strategy on the sideline.

note, it was important for him to complete his academic pursuits, as well. Graduation was a priority, not only for himself, but for his late mother. "That was one of the things my mom wanted me to do," he remembers with a smile. "Actually, she didn't really care about basketball. She enjoyed it because I enjoyed it. When she passed away, all of my attention and focus was on getting my degree, so that I have done right by her, and I feel good about that for myself."

• • •

Michael Jordan, James Worthy, Sam Perkins, and Jimmy Black are all in the same room. The fact that Jordan, Worthy, and Perkins are playing basketball on television and Jimmy is watching is a minor detail. He scrutinizes. He yells. He laughs. He wishes he were out there with them. He had a shot at pro ball, but came up short. Trying to put that experience into perspective, Jimmy recalls, "Initially, it was very disappointing, because after experiencing so much success on the basketball court, now all of a sudden your basketball is taken away from you. It was disappointing."

Disappointing for obvious reasons, but disappointing for other reasons, as well. "I just wanted an opportunity to do things for my family financially," he says. "I'm a survivor. I'm going to be OK no →

Black conducts a children's clinic in Charlotte before the Diet Pepsi Tournament of Champions.

matter what happens. But I just wanted to do something special for my family, and I think an NBA salary would have given me an opportunity to do that."

Jimmy had the opportunity to get closer to the NBA recently. He and Doherty traveled to Chicago for the NBA Finals featuring his former teammates Jordan, Worthy, and Perkins. NBC flew them there to appear at halftime with Bob Costas. The starting five together again. It was a special moment for Jimmy, but something was missing. "I was disappointed that the whole '82 team couldn't come out," he says. "I think that we all shared in something special. I was happy that I was able to go out and express my views, but I think it would have been more special to me to have that whole group together."

Jimmy's time is still spent in basketball, but it is coaching that is his future. He has learned much since his playing days. A different side of basketball was taught to him during his six years as an assistant at St. Joseph's University in Philadelphia. It was not the high profile program of Carolina, but it was a learning situation. A place to take in as much as he could, and then move onward and upward.

He's Coach Black now. Not Jimmy. Not J.B. Not Boss. Not Freddy. Coach Black. Gone are the names that Jimmy Black answered to at Carolina. North Carolina, that is. An assistant's job at the University of South Carolina was the next stop of his basketball career.

He settled in to quiet Columbia, S.C., to try and move up to the next level of his career. "My long-term goal would be to run my own program, to do things the right way, and to try to help any young man I coach to have a fond college experience," he says. "If I can do that, then I think that I will have done my job well."

Jimmy is moving closer to where he wants to be. Big-time college basketball. "It was more challenging," he explains. "It was a larger program. A lot more publicity. A lot more people saw what you were doing, so you were held accountable for a lot more."

It wasn't North Carolina, but it was close. "It was good for me to be back in this area," he admits. "I was happy to be there. I think I had one of the best jobs in the country." →

While at South Carolina, Jimmy had the opportunity to go up against the "other" Carolina. That occasion happened at a tournament in Charlotte. It was billed "The Rivalry Renews." South Carolina versus North Carolina. But it was a rather unpleasant homecoming of sorts for Jimmy. "It was strange, it was strange," he says, speaking softly. "Seeing those blue uniforms run up and down, and have to pull against them, was probably the weirdest experience I've ever had in basketball. Don't get me wrong, I was pulling for South Carolina, because that's where I worked. But after we won that game, I was also sad because I knew how the North Carolina people felt."

In Jimmy's playing days, after a game, win or loss, meetings and film sessions with Coach Smith would follow. Now things are different. Jimmy smiles as he remembers Coach Smith's parting words... "He came in the locker room and congratulated us and wished us well the rest of the season."

The season did not turn out the way Jimmy had hoped. South Carolina had an 18-5 record and was in the Top 20 midway through the season. But they only won 2 of their last 10 games, finishing 20-13. Head Coach George Felton was fired at the end of the season. And Jimmy was left in limbo. That's when he decided to leave South Carolina behind.

Notre Dame was in need of an assistant coach, and Jimmy saw an opportunity. "I think Notre Dame is a great university," he says. "It presents an interesting

Black yells instructions to South Carolina players. *Photo by Bob Leverone.*

challenge because over the past couple of years they've been down. It's a challenge to try and revive that basketball program.

"On the same note, I'm a little disappointed. I really enjoyed the University of South Carolina. I wish they had made some assurances of me being here. But since they didn't do that, I was forced to explore some other options and I think of the options that were available, Notre Dame happens to be one of the best."

• • •

As the end of one season neared, Jimmy was reminded of the end of another. One that he will never forget. While riding back on the bus to Chapel Hill after winning the national championship, he told his fellow senior teammate and roommate Chris Brust (whom he calls his "sanity" because they shared so many things together) that "this would probably be the last time all of us would be together. We were all on that bus and it was great. That's probably my fondest memory.

"I wish I could just freeze that year and just do it one more time, because there were so many little things that happened that no one knows but us. It was a wonderful experience for me." ■

Black answers questions after an NCAA tournament victory.

11

Matt Doherty

"I was appreciated for doing those little things. It didn't get me any sneaker contracts or any million-dollar contracts in the NBA, but it got me an NCAA championship."

Hometown: East Meadow, N.Y.
Height: 6-8
Weight: 210
Class: Sophomore

Matt Doherty walks into Belk Gymnasium, on the campus of Davidson College in Davidson, N.C., a few minutes before tip-off. Someone in the stands calls his name. He steps over and signs an autograph. Someone else pushes a business card in his hand. Matt smiles and thanks him. He puts the card in his pocket. On this basketball court, his uniform is a suit, not the cotton mesh of his old Carolina number 44. He looks in charge. His role is assistant coach. Nothing flashy, nothing glamorous. But fans still remember Matt

---

HE FOUND himself on a basketball court at every spare moment. He dreamed of making it in the NBA. His mind said 'yes,' but his back injury said 'no.' But he knew he was comfortable with basketball; knew he belonged to it. Wall Street wasn't his NBA. Coaching was.

Doherty. Not Matt Doherty, assistant coach for the Davidson Wildcats basketball team. But Matt Doherty, starting forward for the North Carolina Tar Heels.

"I'm surprised that people remember me, especially young kids," Matt says. "It's not really a tribute to me, but a tribute to Dean Smith. Because of the success he's had, I reap some rewards. Whether a reward is signing an autograph or not, I don't know, but it's nice.

"It doesn't matter where it is. I was on I-95, going to D.C. the other day, at a Hardee's getting lunch. This trucker comes in and looks at me, and says, 'Are you Matt Doherty?' and I said, 'Yeah.' He said, 'I'm from Rocky Mount and I enjoyed watching you play.' "

• • •

The first thing Matt asks when told he was mentioned in a *Sports Illustrated* article is, "Did they spell it right?" Not often is a player like Doherty remembered, whether he was a member of a championship team or not. Role players usually do not grab headlines. Role players are not stars. But Matt's name keeps coming up. *Sports Illustrated.* CBS. The local newspaper. He was the consummate role player. "I'd be lying if I told you it didn't feel good," says Matt. "I think everyone's got an ego, and everyone likes to see their name in print, so it does feel good." But he is the first one to deflect attention from himself.

"I think being a role player is like dating your sister," he explains. "There's nothing sexy to it, there's nothing exciting to it, but it was my role. Hey, I wasn't going to shoot the ball more than Michael Jordan or James Worthy or Sam Perkins. That would have been foolish, because they could score a lot easier than I could. So I knew if I wanted to play, I had to do the little things, and that I could do well. Now is that important to the average fan? No. But it was pretty darn →

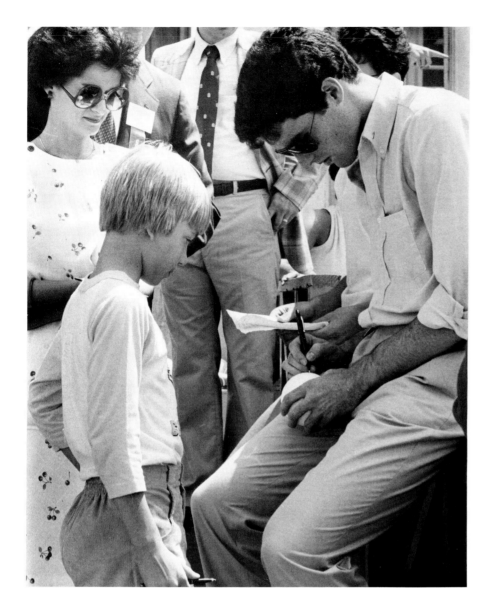

Matt Doherty handles the ball against James Madison, North Carolina's first opponent in the 1982 NCAA tournament (below). At left, Doherty signs autographs after the team returns to Chapel Hill as national champions.

important to Coach Smith, I felt. Obviously it resulted in a lot of minutes and we won, so I was very happy with my career. I enjoyed distributing the basketball. I enjoyed playing defense. I enjoyed winning."

As important as winning was to Matt, there was more to gain from college than just basketball. Camaraderie. Personal relationships. "I don't think you develop bonds with individuals in any other area like you do in athletics," Matt says, "because you have a common goal and you work towards that goal. There are many ups and downs during the course of the year. Wins. Losses. Games that you win that you shouldn't have won. Games that you lose that you shouldn't have lost. So it's like a roller coaster."

The roller coaster ended after Matt's four years at Carolina. He was drafted by the Cleveland Cavaliers. He went to Cleveland, tried out, injured his back and left. He was hurt in more ways than one.

"It was very difficult," he says now. "I equate it to your girlfriend or your wife leaving you, because, to me, basketball was a great part of me, and to have someone tell you, 'You can't play anymore,' it hurt. I was bitter and I wanted to get as far away from basketball as I could. I went to Wall Street and I thought that was a cool thing to do, a sexy thing to do. That was my NBA. So, when people would say 'What do you do now?' I could proudly say, 'I work on Wall Street.' "

But being a stockbroker turned out to be less than glamorous. "I really didn't feel comfortable with what I was doing and who I was," he recalls.

He found himself on a basketball court at every spare moment. He dreamed of making it in the NBA. His mind said "yes," but his back injury said "no." But he knew he was comfortable with basketball; knew he belonged to it. Wall Street wasn't his NBA. Coaching was. ➔

13

Doherty and Michael Jordan take a break from the action.

"I know more about basketball than anything else," he says. "I've been working at basketball since I was in the fourth grade, and I haven't been doing anything else that long. That's what I know, and I feel like I can talk on a knowledgeable level to anybody about it. I think I have opinions that I believe in, because I've played, and I try to be a student of the game."

The first stop on the road back to basketball was a talk with Dean Smith. "Coach Smith would say to me, 'Are you prepared to go to Montana?'" remembers Matt, "and I looked at him, like wow, I didn't think of that. Not that Montana's a bad place, but being from the East Coast, you may want to stay around a little bit. And then he said, 'You won't have any free weekends. It's very time-consuming.'"

The second stop wasn't Montana. As fate would

have it, Matt's high school coach, Bob McKillop, had been hired as head coach at Davidson College in May of 1989. He needed an assistant. Matt needed a job and jumped at the opportunity. "Bob McKillop is like working with a friend," he says.

"I think basketball coaches, the successful ones, work harder than anybody in any other profession. People may think I'm crazy, but the hours you keep, the frustration you have to deal with ... a lot of it is out of your control. It's different things thrown in your lap every day. But I enjoy what I'm doing, I really do like it. It's a great opportunity for me to be at Davidson. In the world of athletics today, where there seems to be a great imbalance between academics and athletics, Davidson is a very good mix. It's a great place. It's a place I believe in." →

14

Doherty, now an assistant coach at Davidson College in Davidson, N.C., instructs a Wildcat player. *Photo by Bob Leverone.*

But believing in something and making it work are two different things, which Matt has accepted. Many obstacles stand in the way of becoming a successful college coach. The long hours. The job insecurity. The losing.

"I don't think anybody has job security, whether it's coaching, or real estate, or Wall Street," Matt says. "We're losing in terms of on the court, but I see a lot of winning going on. I see a lot of growth. I see an exciting future. That, to me, is fun. The building process is very challenging. I like challenges.

"I feel if I'm suited to do anything in this world, it's to coach basketball. I really do. I believe that. I feel I know the game. I can deal with people. I like dealing with kids. I like the P.R. part of it. I like talking on the telephone. I like hunting down players ... it's like a detective. I like traveling. I like the different schedule, because I get bored if I'm sitting in one place too long. I like scouting. I like all that, so I feel real lucky to have

a job I feel is tailor-made for me."

Tailor-made, the way his position at North Carolina was. Players are compared to Matt Doherty. He likes that. Role player. He likes that, too.

"I've been very fortunate throughout my career, in grammar school, high school, and college, to win championships," he says. "It's been fun. I really envision myself coaching a championship team. That's exciting to me. I'm not satisfied, I'm happy. I'm excited because I feel I'm pursuing the dream, not just a goal."

Just like the dream of winning the national championship in 1982. After the game was over, the ceremonies completed, Matt stood on the court, holding a piece of the net.

"I felt like I didn't deserve the whole net. I think James or Jimmy deserved that. But I wanted a piece of it and I wasn't going to let it go!" ■

Michael Jordan

"I think it initiated all the following success that I have had. I think if you take that away, there's no telling if I would be in the same situation."

Hometown: Wilmington, N.C.
Height: 6-5
Weight: 189
Class: Freshman

Even with all his awards and accolades, Michael Jordan still considers the 1982 NCAA national championship one of his greatest achievements, the start of a snowball that continues rolling downhill.

"Mainly because it propelled my career to where I achieved all these other things ... where I had the confidence to achieve all these other things," he says. "If you take that away, I don't think I could have had that."

Michael actually narrows the national championship down to the shot. Everyone who saw the game remembers that shot. Seventeen seconds left. Michael

---

MICHAEL ACCEPTS the loss of privacy that such creativity and skill have brought him, but he admits that he sometimes tires of the attention and longs to come and go as he did in the old days.

---

from the left wing. Swish. Everybody who saw it knew that it was going in. Even Michael.

"Ever since I made that shot, everything has just fallen into place for me," he says. "Everything has been perfect. It was destiny. If that shot hadn't gone in, I don't think I would be where I am today."

Now, of course, Michael is with the Chicago Bulls, the 1991 NBA champions, and he is the primary reason they are champions.

"This is something that has been a seven-year struggle for me," he says. "We started from scratch. We

hadn't made the playoffs in a couple of years, and I vowed that as long as I was with the team we were certainly going to make the playoffs.

"And each year we got closer and closer. We plugged and plugged. I saw each level of getting closer to the championship and the light was still there. I never gave up hope. I always had faith that I was going to get it one day. It took seven years but I'm happy I got it."

His teammates are happy, too. Michael makes everyone around him better, but he was glad to see his teammates finally emerge from his shadow in the '91 Finals.

"It should get rid of the stigma of being a one-man team," he says. "We have players surrounding myself that make us an effective basketball team. Now my teammates have stepped up, and the stigma is removed."

Although much of the team's success is due to Michael, success, if not handled properly, he says, can cloud ambitions and goals.

"Success is something that can overwhelm you," he says. "I think it's something that I certainly pay attention to, so that it won't overwhelm me and change me as a person. If you go out and search for success, you never really get it. It's one of those things, that you just go out, and you work hard, and you try to achieve certain things, and let things happen the way they are going to happen." →

Michael Jordan takes flight in preparation for a slam dunk.

Jordan cuts down the net in New Orleans after North Carolina won the 1982 NCAA championship.

However, society, he says, can sometimes dictate success.

"Society seeks personalities," he continues. "It's amazing what society can do to one individual that makes him stand above most people. It just falls upon you when you least expect it."

What many people, including Michael, didn't expect was the impact he would have at Carolina. Everyone knew he was a good player, but all eyes were on Buzz Peterson. Buzz had won the North Carolina High School Basketball Player of the Year Award from the Associated Press and was impressive at many all-star camps. It was at one of these camps that Michael and Buzz made an agreement. "Buzz and I were a pack-

age deal," he remembers. "We just decided, then and there, that we were going to go to the same school."

Peterson has told that story before, and he says people laugh and think he is joking when they hear it. He convinces them that it is indeed true, then goes on to explain what he saw in Michael.

"Michael was playing a lot of different sports (in high school)," he says. "He was a very good baseball player and he could throw the football. He just had to concentrate on one sport. When we got to school, he played (basketball) every day. I knew he was going to be a big player. It was going to be enjoyable just playing with him."

"I was nervous when I first got to Carolina," →

18

Jordan was a member of the 1984 U.S. Olympic basketball team, which won the gold medal. During training for the Games, the Olympic team played an exhibition game against an NBA all-star team. James Worthy, visible in background here, was a member of that NBA team.

Michael says. "I was treated just like every other freshman. I had to carry the film projector, chase after the loose balls. Buzz was more of the star when we started school. There wasn't much pressure on me then."

Michael took advantage of the lack of spotlight, and developed quickly in practice. So quickly, in fact, that he started in the first game of his freshman year.

"When I saw my name up on the board to start," he says, "I couldn't believe it. I was nervous. But I went out and made the first shot, and started to settle down."

Settle down, he did. He made the first shot of the season and the already-mentioned last shot. He also continued to develop his skills while at Carolina. Matt Doherty remembers Jordan's progression. "I remem-

ber after practice one day, we were playing chicken, where each guy would take the ball at the hash mark, and dribble in, and the other guy would try to block it, and you would try to dunk. I remember him dunking on me, but I remember dunking on him. That changed quickly. I didn't want to play chicken after his freshman year. He really grew up, physically and mentally. His game really expanded between his freshman and sophomore years. He became a man."

• • •

In Charlotte in the spring of 1991, Michael is sitting in his hotel suite. His friends mingle, playing cards, watching TV, talking. Michael is trying to eat a few bites before he leaves for the arena. There are →

19

Even on the sidelines, Jordan keeps his eye on the game.

people out in the hall, strangers, waiting to see him as he leaves, hoping to touch him, get his autograph. In college he could come and go as he pleased. Now he needs help, security agents, backdoors, private exits. But he understands.

"I enjoy people, I like being around people," he says. "My jumping ability has a lot of creativity and it adds to the admiration of most fans, because fans like the dunk, they like the creative things."

That creativity couldn't have been more evident than in the '91 NBA Finals. Michael had always been known for the shot in 1982, but he will also be remembered for another shot in 1991. Driving the lane in Game 2, he appeared to be headed for one of his trademark right-handed slams, but instead, he switched the ball to his left hand, laying in a perfectly timed, spinning, reverse bank shot. "I was going to dunk the ball when I saw the long-armed Perkins there," he explains. "I exposed the ball for him, and just by instinct, I put it in my left hand. It's one of those creative things. Sometimes, with creativity, you don't know what's going to happen. Not in my game, anyway."

Michael accepts the loss of privacy that such creativity and skill have brought him, but he admits that he sometimes tires of the attention and longs to come

and go as he did in the old days, before he became so famous. "I go through my periods of just being tired of doing everything, everybody grabbing at you, but everybody goes through a moody period. I've been able to separate the two and get my relaxation when I need it."

One way he has tried to escape attention, ironically, is by going out more, dropping in at the mall, taking in a movie. "You have to start doing these things that your family wants to do," he says, "even though you have to put up with a little more. For the most part, it's gone smoothly. I think, as I continue to get out, and people start to see me out, then it's going to be more of an acceptance. People won't say, 'Let's get his autograph, because we may not see him out anymore.' Nowadays, you get to see me out there quite a bit."

There are times when he relishes being in the spotlight off the court, and that is when he makes appearances for various charities. "I don't have to do it, but it's a sense of giving something back," he says. "I've been very fortunate to get to where I am, in a short amount of time, and to do it in a different style than most people. So, I almost feel obligated to give something back, and I do that through the charitable things that I do.   →

"It's a good feeling that I get, from my presence and my conversation with people. They take it and it makes a big difference in their lives ... That means a lot."

• • •

Dean Smith made a big difference in Michael Jordan's life. "He teaches more than basketball, he teaches you about life," Michael says, "about just being a part of society. He can do no wrong. Not in my book. Because he's done so much right for me. And he's always very caring about the player as a person, not a basketball player, a person."

There's a worn-out joke about Smith being the only person to hold Jordan under 20 points a game. It makes Michael shake his head. "I wouldn't be where I am today without Coach Smith. I learned defense, how to block out, everything under him. I learned all the little things you need to be successful on and off the basketball court. He's a second father to many, not just myself, to many."

Michael is now learning firsthand about fatherhood. He and his wife, Juanita, are the parents of two sons, Jeffrey and Marcus. Michael has been kidded about having a future backcourt with his sons, but he's not so sure. "I'm not going to try and push them towards basketball, they don't have to follow in my footsteps," he says. Whatever they choose to do, Michael plans to teach them the lessons he learned from Smith: set goals and strive to reach them.

Sometimes Michael wonders what he might have done had he not chosen basketball.

"I always feel that every time I look at baseball or football players, I can stop right now playing basketball, and go play one of those sports," he says.

MICHAEL TREASURES the familiar: old friends, family, home. He always looks forward to coming back to North Carolina. His parents are in Charlotte now, making it even more fun when the Bulls visit the Hornets.

"That's how much confidence I have in my abilities to pick up things quickly."

He remembers a time in Chapel Hill when the entire basketball team was playing football on a snow-covered parking lot in front of their dorm. Naturally, he

With the Chicago Bulls, Jordan has reached new pinnacles, including an NBA championship.

was the quarterback. "Those times," he says, "that's when I really experimented and excited myself about playing different sports. To throw the touchdown, to get the sense of being a football player. To see what they must go through. I understand those feelings. One of these days I may just quit and go play another professional sport just to see what the challenge is."

That challenge may come sooner than later. Michael has made no secret of his desire to play professional golf after he hangs up his famous footwear. He tries to play now in every spare moment, rain or shine. "Once I get out on the course," he says, "I know no one is going to come out and bother me. It's very relaxing. It helps me deal with myself, mentally. It totally gets me away from basketball but still gives me that competitive drive that I need. Playing golf is great for me. That's where I can be normal."

His only other chance for normalcy, apart from his family, comes from hanging out with friends. They treat him as a regular guy, not a superstar.

To his friends, he's Mike, Air, or MJ. Michael marks his different names as progressions in his career, viewing each as a level of maturity, growth and respect "Mike Jordan started out as an unknown," he says →

with a grin. "Then it became Michael Jordan when I made that shot and we got the national championship." After the Olympics, "Air" was added to his name. Nikes, billboards, commercials followed. Now it is simply MJ to those who have known him for years. "It's just more familiar," he says.

Michael treasures the familiar: old friends, family, home. He always looks forward to coming back to North Carolina. His parents are in Charlotte now, making it even more fun when the Bulls visit the Hornets. "It's fun to be around people, my guys, and to spend some time with them," he says. "I go a long time without seeing them, and it's always great to see them. It's tough trying to get tickets for everybody. That situation is always a headache, but I don't care how many times I come, how many times I'm away, it's always great to come back home."

• • •

In all probability, Michael won't come back home to North Carolina after he no longer can fly and dunk with ease on the basketball court.

"I'm certainly going to try to step away from the spotlight as much as possible, and try to settle back down into a normal life, if I can. My home is still going to be in Chicago, because of my family situation. But it's cold up there. I want to go somewhere normal. Probably San Diego is where we'll go and spend a lot of time. The weather is great. The privacy to a certain extent. You can be somewhat of a normal person."

Does he still keep in touch with Buzz Peterson?

"Yes. We were just like brothers in college, and it's continued. I wear my sweatband high on my arm to remind me of Buzz. He messed up his knee (in college). He had the same attitude about basketball that I had, and I actually could understand what he was going through with that injury. I just wanted to show what he meant to me, and that he was a part of me every mtime I stepped on the basketball court. I still wear it now. And he knows it. It means a lot to me, and he's going to be with me as long as I play the game."

What about those Carolina shorts he always wears?

"It started when I first went to professional ball. It got to the point in my rookie season where I missed college, and all the things that you learn through that system, and all the unity that went on with being a part of that team. So I just said, 'Hey, I'll put these shorts on,' and it gives me a good sense of home, a good

Jordan says he would like to become a professional golfer when his basketball days are over.

remembrance. And now it's like a piece of my clothing. I don't go anywhere without them. That means I'm carrying a piece of North Carolina wherever I go. It really makes me feel at home. I wear them everywhere I go -- under suits, pants, shorts, my uniform – everywhere. Carolina sends me a new supply every year."

What was it like having four former Tar Heels in the 1991 NBA Finals?

"Even though they tried to make it a →

22

Magic/Michael situation, what made it for me was playing against James and Sam, and also that Scott (Williams) was on the team. That was special, four guys from a very solid program, and yet we were competing, two on each team."

How does the 1991 NBA championship compare to the 1982 NCAA championship?

"It was a different situation when I went to the Bulls as opposed to when I went to Carolina. At Carolina I jumped into a situation where there were other stars. I kind of walked into an established situation. Winning as a freshman, I didn't have a sense of how important it was, how difficult it was, because we just won it right away.

"In this situation, the NBA championship, I started from the bottom and worked my way up. It's a little bit more gratifying to see those stages, than to actually just walk in and win it, but both of them were happy moments."

Why all the uncharacteristic emotion after winning the NBA championship?

"No one likes to show emotion a lot, especially myself. I've never been able to do that, not publicly. When I look back it's really touching. No matter what level you're on, you still feel that youth, those emotions of youth, and sometimes you show it. I guess it was a happy moment. I just could not hold back on my emotions. So many times I've been in front of a camera and dealt with the press and been able to control my emotions. But this one time I couldn't do it. I was a crybaby for once, but it was a great time to be a crybaby. I don't know if I'll ever have that same feeling." ■

Jordan goes to the basket against Georgetown's Patrick Ewing in the 1982 NCAA championship game.

Sam Perkins

"I didn't realize what we had accomplished until we got back and saw the state that the people of North Carolina and Chapel Hill were in."

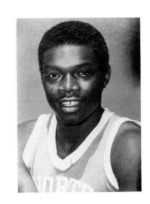

Hometown: Latham, N.Y.
Height: 6-9
Weight: 224
Class: Sophomore

Sam Perkins sometimes tries to imagine if the Tar Heels hadn't won the 1982 national championship game. "If we had lost, you would have had so many people knocking the stuffing out of their couches and pillows," he says.

Lucky for Sam and fans' furniture, it was Carolina knocking in the shots that led the Tar Heels to their first national basketball title since 1957 and made Carolina fans so joyous and appreciative.

"We had a strong group, from Jimmy to Matt, to

EVEN THOUGH he has won an NCAA championship, a Pan Am gold medal, an Olympic gold medal, and is beginning a six-year contract that pays him more than $3 million a year, Sam still has dreams.

---

the guys on the bench," he says. "Everybody was instrumental."

Sam still speaks in that same soft tone, still maintains the same calm demeanor he exhibited in the 1982 NCAA Final Four. He scored 25 points and hauled down 10 rebounds to lead the Tar Heels to victory against Houston in the semifinals. That was a Houston team with Clyde Drexler and Akeem Olajuwon. Many people have long forgotten that game and Sam's dominance of it, and even Sam can't remember much about it. "We were facing a lot of guys like Clyde and

Olajuwon, who was just a freshman at the time," he recalls. "We had to come out and just take care of ourselves. I was just trying to play. It seemed like ... I kind of forget about that game."

What he hasn't forgotten is those tense tournament days in New Orleans. "There were people all over from Georgetown, Louisville, Houston, and us. Those things really kind of stand out in my mind, not necessarily the game, but all the things before and after. It was kind of nerve-wracking, sitting in your room anticipating the game to come. Losing one year (in 1981 against Indiana) and then coming back to win it all was a great accomplishment for us."

Despite that accomplishment, Sam's place in basketball was not so certain after he left Carolina. A six-year stop with the Dallas Mavericks left him wondering about his future. Would he ever again be the star he was in college? Would he ever experience another championship? Could he get used to losing in the NBA?

"At Dallas, we lost six of our first seven, and no one thought anything of it," he recalls. "I would come back in the locker room feeling all disappointed and hurt. Everyone else came in and they felt bad, but there was a game the next day, so, I had to wake up to that feeling. Everybody else could accept losing, but I couldn't. After awhile, it just grew on me. This is the lifestyle of the NBA, and you just don't worry about one game." →

Sam Perkins views the action on the court under the watchful eye of Dean Smith.

Despite the losses, the Mavericks were full of potential. "Dallas was a city that was up and coming, and the team was exciting because we had the ability to move on, to grow, to be a contender," Sam says. "Eventually we did, but we kind of, as they say, over-achieved, and we never really peaked when we should have."

The team may not have peaked at the right time, but Sam continued to climb, and established himself as one of the best all-around players on the Mavericks. During his Dallas days, he caught the eye of NBA team owners throughout the league. His reputation for tough defense, rebounding, and hard work took him from the concrete and glass of Dallas to the sun and fun of Los Angeles, land of golden dreams.

Even though he has won an NCAA championship, a Pan Am gold medal, an Olympic gold medal,

and is beginning a six-year contract that pays him more than $3 million a year, Sam still has dreams. And that wide Perkins smile emerges as he talks about them.

The first is obvious: an NBA championship. That was why he chose the Los Angeles Lakers as the team on which to complete his career. More money was available at lesser teams, but not the opportunity to play for a contender. "Out of all those teams, they were the closest to winning a championship somewhere in the near future," Sam says.

Also the Lakers offered the opportunity to play again with his old college friend and teammate, James Worthy. "James and I were close in college, and we went our separate ways, but we still kept in contact," Sam says. "Now that we are here, we've grown to like each other a great deal. We still have that camaraderie that we had in college, but we live our own lives and →

25

Perkins shoots for two over Patrick Ewing of Georgetown in the 1982 NCAA championship game.

give each other room, yet we do hang out and talk a lot."

Worthy is familiar with Sam's second dream: to be an NBA All-Star. Although Sam is one of the most consistent players in the league, he has failed to make an All-Star team in his seven-year career. "I would probably have to do twice as much," Sam says.

Although Sam feels that he may have work harder to get noticed on a team loaded with superstars, he has established himself as an integral component of the Lakers as they continue their winning ways.

"I would like to reach different and new heights, and would love to be in the superstar status," Sam acknowledges. "But for what I do now, I would rather pass it to James, make a good rebound, or do something defensively to make the difference. But now coaches are saying I need to be a little more selfish. I just try to do everything I can, whether it's passing, shooting, →

26

rebounding, to make it complete for me, to know I am satisfied."

That brings us to dream number three, as in the 3-Point Contest held during the All-Star Weekend festivities. Sam's desire to participate in this long-range shootout originated when opponents began to fear his 3-point accuracy at Carolina. Yes, the 3-point line in college is closer to the basket than the one in the pros, but his success and confidence with launching "treys" in the NBA was evidenced by his game-winning 3-pointer in Game 1 of the 1991 NBA Finals against Jordan and the Chicago Bulls.

"When I left the bench, I turned to Mike (Coach Dunleavy) and asked if he wanted me to spot up at the 3-point line," Sam said. "He said 'Yeah,' so I took that to mean take it if it's there."

Although Coach Dunleavy admitted he, in fact, did not mean for Sam to shoot the 3-pointer, none of the Lakers minded when they saw the ball pass through the net. However, Jordan and the Bulls minded. "Sam made a heck of a 3-point shot to win it," Jordan said, "and the team that makes the big plays down the stretch is going to win. It took a North Carolina guy to beat me, though."

Sam hopes to continue that success in future seasons, and plant himself not only behind the 3-point line during the regular season, but at the All-Star Weekend, as well.

Just three dreams. Sam doesn't think that's too much. "That would be all the things I would want," he says, "before I would finally leave this game. Just to satisfy me, so I could say, 'Well, I did just about everything I could.' "

• • •

Sam calls Worthy and Jordan great players, but doesn't include himself in that category. That's why he chose to stay in school instead of leaving early for the NBA draft. "My game plan was to stay four years," he says. And about that he has no regrets.

"Carolina really prepared me for some things I wasn't wise about and am still learning about," he says. "Those are things where you lay down the groundwork for life after basketball."

He gives Dean Smith the credit for stressing the importance of values beyond basketball. "He gives you room to grow and to have responsibility," Sam says. "He really didn't want to spoon feed you, because he wasn't there to babysit, but at the same time he gave us direction and sat down with us all the time. Basketball wasn't the only thing he wanted us to do well. I   →

Sam Perkins joined Michael Jordan on the 1984 Olympic Team, which played an exhibition game in the Greensboro Coliseum.

Now playing for the Los Angeles Lakers, Perkins takes a break during a game against the Charlotte Hornets in Charlotte.

enjoy playing. I like it a lot. But I know it's not going to be here forever.

"Coach Smith told me basketball is probably a minute fraction of what you really have to do after basketball. I took it like that, and with that advice, that's how I live now."

That's why Sam may eventually seek a career in his college major, communications. "Maybe radio, owning a radio station," he says. After all, one of Sam's favorite pastimes is listening to music. He carries a portable CD player wherever he goes. "It's relaxing. I need music all the time, just to cool out with." But Sam has other hobbies, as well: fishing, tennis, traveling. "I do different things, go to different places just to make sure my summers are not the same," he says.

Still, basketball dominates his life for now, and despite the loss of the 1991 NBA championship, he feels good about his situation, especially about playing again with Worthy.

"When we lead in scoring or do something similar in a game, it's like 'Sam Perkins and James Worthy did this,' " he says with a smile. "That brings back college memories when we had the headlines then. It's just funny how things worked out. You play with somebody and go away for awhile, and return to do the same thing in a different situation, place, and time.

"It just gives you a pretty nice feeling that Carolina dished out a brand of guys that possibly any one of us could be playing together at any time. Just to see that life kind of evolves around a little bit. That's special." ■

28

James Worthy

"The intensity just seemed to explode at the right time. It was almost like a miracle for it to happen that way. It was like a book, an ending to a book."

Hometown: Gastonia, N.C.
Height: 6-9
Weight: 219
Class: Junior

Well, not quite the ending, for James Worthy is still writing his book. A book on how to succeed.

James' ambition, as recorded in the 1982 North Carolina media guide, was "to be successful in whatever I do."

"I've accomplished a lot of things," he says, "and if that's the gauge for success, I feel like I've done that."

His story is well known now: MVP in the 1982 NCAA championship game; drafted No. 1 by the Los

THERE IS MUCH more to James Worthy than accolades and championships. A private, quiet man lurks behind the clear, plastic goggles he sports on game nights. He seeks no limelight, wanting only to be James. And that can be hard to do in a city like Los Angeles

Angeles Lakers after leaving UNC at the end of his junior year; NBA championships with the Lakers in 1985, '87, and '88; MVP of the 1988 playoffs.

James has a reputation for excelling in the big games. His best game in college was his final one against Georgetown, and it's no coincidence that his play continues to improve whenever the Lakers enter the NBA playoffs.

Matt Doherty recognized this trait early on. "I think he was just bored with the lesser teams," says

Matt. "In the big games, no one played better than James. In those games – Kentucky in the Meadowlands, Virginia in the ACC Tournament, obviously Georgetown in the finals – he was a man among boys."

But there is much more to James Worthy than accolades and championships. A private, quiet man lurks behind the clear, plastic goggles he sports on game nights. He seeks no limelight, no spotlight, wanting only to be James. And that can be hard to do in a city like Los Angeles.

James did not choose Los Angeles. Los Angeles chose him. Not that he is complaining. He just didn't want to be a celebrity. He didn't consider himself a celebrity at Chapel Hill. "Everybody knew you were a basketball player, but it was easy to fit in," he says. "I didn't feel like I stood out that much, that I wasn't a part of the rest of the student body."

Los Angeles brims with celebrities, though, and if you star for the Lakers, the spotlight shines on you, whether you like it or not.

"I don't seek it, but sometimes it's hard to avoid it," James says. "I accepted it a long time ago, and learned how to deal with it because it's part of the job. But sometimes it's hard to take that attitude. Sometimes you don't want to deal with it at all, especially in certain situations. But for the most part, you have to accept it and keep on walking. Never stop walking....   →

29

James Worthy looks to pass the ball against Georgetown during the 1982 NCAA championship game.

"It's a lot better now, but it was different in the beginning, making adjustments from North Carolina to the big city. It gets better as the years go by."

As the years have gone by, James has harbored no regrets about his decision to leave Carolina early. "I think I made the right move," he says. "The timing was right. It was a situation where Ralph Sampson wasn't coming out, and that enhanced my draft situation. I was able to go first (in the draft), so I was able to end up with the Lakers."

But he left without finishing his degree, and he does not like to leave things unfinished. "It's crucial, because early on in college, all you think about is graduate on time, graduate on time," he says. "Then if you leave early, you get into a financial situation where you forget about that goal of graduating on time. You forget about graduating, period. So, it's tougher to come back. But for some reason, Coach Smith and the whole academic program have something to do with that (getting you to come back). They're encouraging you, and it says something about you, too, that you can come back. Coming back and finishing up in '85 really made it complete, like bookends. I think it definitely was the right move."

Not all James' moves have been right. Some have been wrong, though not by choice. Like one move toward the basket during his freshman year, when he stepped on a piece of ice and then suddenly found himself lying on the court of Carmichael Auditorium with a broken ankle. A couple of years later, he lay on the floor of the Forum in Los Angeles with a fractured tibia. Although the injuries were a few years and a few thousand miles apart, both had the same message to James: "Wake up!"

James considers the first injury in college as a blessing in disguise. "At the time, I was really into basketball," he says. "I was forgetting what my purpose was. You get off track sometime, particularly a young guy coming to college. The time that I wasn't with the team, I was hanging out with the guys on the floor. I really got a chance to see a more realistic view of what college was all about. I got a chance to communicate with a lot of students who weren't athletes. That helped me set my priorities a lot better."

And even though James was prepared to deal with the physical ramifications of his injury in the pros, he encountered the same mental anquish he had gone through years earlier. "You don't know whether you're going to be able to move like you used to," he says. "Your occupation, your salary depends on how →

30

Worthy and Smith relax after the 1982 championship game.

healthy your body is in this business. It (an injury) does something to you emotionally, if you aren't prepared for it."

James has always bounced back from his injuries, although recurring back soreness sidelines him from time to time, and the sprained ankle he suffered in the 1991 NBA Finals slowed him and the Lakers down. Still he remains one of the most consistent players in the league. Just as he was in college.

There was one major change for James when he moved from college to professional basketball.

"You feel alone. You're out there against the world. You're responsible. You don't have a roommate anymore. You miss the family."

James set about dealing with these matters in his own quiet way.

First he married Angela Wilder, a former Carolina cheerleader. They now have a daughter, Sable Alexandria. "Being married is a challenge and so is having a child," James admits. "It's a big responsi- ➔

Worthy left North Carolina after his junior year and joined the Los Angeles Lakers of the NBA, where he became a teammate of Kareem Abdul-Jabbar (below).

bility and one of the biggest challenges in the world."

A smile crosses James' lips when he mentions his own parents, who reared him in Gastonia.

"A lot of their values are my values. I've always been able to be open with them. They're just genuine people. There are times that I didn't agree with them, but later on I learned that they were right. I'm still the little baby knucklehead," he says with a laugh.

Ervin Worthy, James' father, worked three jobs to support the family when James and his brothers were growing up.

Mr. Worthy now watches his son on television and marvels at it. "I see him, and I never would have thought that I could see my own child on television doing the things he's doing. It's a blessing. I told him that the same talent God gave him, he could take it away from him right quick if he didn't stay humble and recognize where his blessing came from."

Whenever James returns to North Carolina, people ask if he still thinks of it as home. His answer is always much the same. "As long as my parents are here, I'll always come back. I'm probably going to stay in L.A. a while. I've lived all of my adult life there."

Usually accompanying the question of home comes the one about life after basketball. James is

uncomfortable with that one, because he doesn't see himself leaving the game anytime soon. "Hopefully, between now and the time I retire, I'll decide what I would like to do," he says. "We get the opportunity to try different entrepreneural-type things. I'd like to hope that I can monitor what I invest properly, and use that as a tool to learn about financing, real estate, taxes, whatever. So when the time comes to take over that, I'll be prepared. Hopefully, I won't have to make that decision too quickly.

"I play basketball, but I'm not one-dimensional by any means. I've never had the opportunity to pursue anything else. I've always been focused on basketball, so when that time comes, it will be interesting."

Until then, James hopes to continue doing what he does best. "I've been fortunate enough to win some championships, and once you get that feeling, you always strive for that. I love the game, regardless of how much complaining: the long schedule, how sore you are, the business side of it. You still have that feeling when you go out there, the competitiveness of it. I think that's what keeps me going. We're still the playground kings of yesterday." ■

THEN AND NOW

The starting five on the 1982 Tar Heels team are still very much involved in basketball. The national championship wasn't their last game, because these guys are still with the game, either playing or coaching.

James Worthy shoots for two against Georgetown in the 1982 NCAA championship game.

Above, Coach Dean Smith signals his team during the championship game against Georgetown. At right, Jimmy Black glides in for a layup

A huddle with Coach Smith
for some quick instructions
during the championship
game.

Jimmy Black and Matt Doherty are still involved in basketball — but as coaches, not players. Black is now an assistant coach at Notre Dame, while Doherty is an assistant at Davidson College. The two met during the 1990 season when Davidson played South Carolina. At the time, Black was an assistant for the Gamecocks. *Photo by Bob Leverone.*

Michael Jordan in a dunk mode during a game against the Charlotte Hornets in 1991. Jordan capped the season by leading the Chicago Bulls to an NBA championship.

37

Jordan signs autographs in Charlotte. He says Charlotte fans, like Carolina fans, are loyal. 'When you come back and play in front of them, they cheer you in warm-ups. But when the game starts they cheer for the home team.'

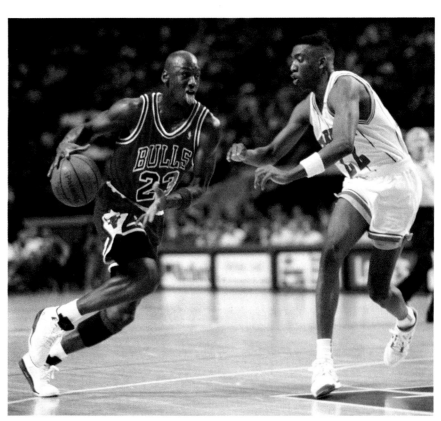

Jordan drives to the basket in action against the Hornets.

At left, Sam Perkins looks to pass against Kelly Tripucka of the Charlotte Hornets during the 1991 NBA season. Below, Perkins joins James Worthy and his father, Ervin, in the locker room after a game.

Above, Worthy drives against Kevin McHale of the Boston Celtics during the 1991 NBA All-Star Game, played in Charlotte. *Photo by Jim Morton.* At right, Worthy prepares to slam unopposed by the Charlotte Hornets.

The Bench

Jeb Barlow
Jim Braddock
John Brownlee
Chris Brust
Cecil Exum

Timo Makkonen
Warren Martin
Buzz Peterson
Lynwood Robinson

Jeb Barlow

"I've got that game on tape and still watch it and wonder sometimes who is going to win."

Hometown: Fuquay-Varina, N.C.
Height: 6-8
Weight: 207
Class: Senior

When Jeb Barlow, the only senior team member who didn't get to play in the championship game, is asked what stands out most about the game, he says it wasn't the victory itself, not Michael hitting the shot, not James stealing the pass.

"We were in the locker room after the game, my dad's in there and we're all celebrating, whooping and hollering," he recalls.

"Coach Smith comes over to me immediately after he gets into the room, before he talks to anybody else. He pulls me to the side and apologizes for not get-

---

JEB JOINED the team his junior year, after playing two years at Louisburg College. The only other junior college player to make a Dean Smith-coached team was Bob McAdoo.

---

ting me in the game. Basically, he was sorry that I didn't get a chance to play in my last college game. I said, 'Coach, we just won the national championship! I couldn't care less if I got in the game or not.' That was his concern at the time, not that he had just won the national championship."

Jeb joined the team his junior year, after playing two years at Louisburg College. The only other junior college player to make a Dean Smith-coached team was Bob McAdoo.

"I was accepted (at Carolina) as a freshman, but

I wanted to try and play basketball (at Louisburg), and see how good I could be," Jeb says.

He believes he made the right decision, using that time to work on his fundamentals and develop physically. He hoped his successful career at Louisburg would open some doors, but found it wasn't that easy.

"It was frustrating at the time to walk on (at Carolina), because I had some scholarship offers from major colleges," he recalls, "and I felt like I had the ability to play major college basketball. Coach Smith didn't really encourage me to come, but he didn't say 'Don't come' either. I didn't have any doubt that if I worked hard, that I could make the team."

It was this attitude that eventually earned Jeb a scholarship after the first two weeks of practice. He also attributes that work ethic to the success of the Tar Heels while he was there. "Just a real positive mental attitude and a winning attitude, knowing that if you work hard, good things will happen."

A good thing did happen, but in a most unusual way. It involved Carolina's final practice before the championship game. Jeb and James Worthy almost got into a scuffle, which led Smith to call practice off. "Coach had told me to push him (Worthy) around a little bit because he knew the Georgetown game was going to be physical," Jeb says. Even with the physical play Jeb was called upon to perform, it was unusual for tempers to flare between Carolina teammates. ➜

But fellow senior Jimmy Black believes that intensity gave the team more confidence as the championship game approached. An inspired Worthy went on to lead Carolina to the championship the next day, and Jeb was cheering him all the way. "James really stepped it up a notch in the tournament," he says. "He just played some outstanding basketball. I think that's what we did that last season. We worked real hard, we played well together. We gelled as a team."

Jeb continued to work hard in basketball after graduation. He traveled to Europe, playing professionally for a team in England. It wasn't glamorous, but he proved he could cut it professionally. His team was successful and so was he.

Unfortunately, not everything off the court was going as well. Contract problems, boredom, and adjustments to the European lifestyle were enough to bring him back home. "It was kind of a transition after the end of my college career to get it out of my system," he says. "I answered the questions that I had, and then realized that I could do this for a few more years, but wasn't ever going to make a bunch of money doing it, or make a living at it. It was a good experience. I decided to go ahead and find a real job and just see what I enjoyed."

Jeb, his wife Marilyn, and their son, Neal, live in Little Rock, Arkansas. Although Jeb is a successful salesman these days, everywhere he goes, basketball follows. "People always ask me, because of my height (6-9), if I played basketball, and then, of course, the next question is where? You tell them you played in '82, and they say, 'Oh, that's the year you won the national championship.' You get automatic notoriety wherever you go. It's kind of nice."

But Jeb enjoys life without basketball. He plays occasional summer and winter leagues, but admits his real game now is golf. "I'm still real competitive and hate to lose," he says. "I've had to transfer some of that competitive nature into my job and golf. Basketball helps keep the spare tire off, but it's kind of frustrating. Your brain says, 'Do what you used to do,' and your body says, 'No.'

"There's just other things I enjoy doing now. Carolina was fun while it lasted, but it's nice to be back in the background, in the shadows." ■

Jeb Barlow goes to the basket against St. Joseph's. Barlow was one of three seniors on the team in 1982. *Photo courtesy of UNC Sports Information Office.*

Jim Braddock

"It was a dream come true. That's why I chose Carolina. I expected us to be in the national championship game."

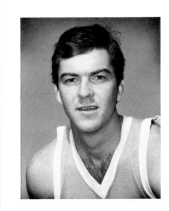

Hometown: Chattanooga, Tenn.
Height: 6-2
Weight: 171
Class: Junior

Expectations sometimes do not turn into reality. But in Jim Braddock's case, they did. Reality was the national championship, and even though Jim may have expected it, he did not take it for granted. He credits hard work and good health as the keys to his and the team's success.

"I pride myself that I was there for four years and I played in every game that I dressed out for, and I dressed out for every game," he says. "I was real fortunate being able to play basketball with the players

---

JIM WAS known as the free spirit on the team. Born and raised in Tennessee, he brought to Chapel Hill a laid-back, relaxed, country attitude that mixed well with the team.

---

and the teams we had. To be able to play every day and not have to sit out because I was hurt was just icing on the cake. That's something that meant a lot to me. Always knowing I was there to participate, to practice hard, and help the team, whether it be in practice or coming in for Jimmy (Black)."

Jim was known as the free spirit on the team. Born and raised in Tennessee, he brought to Chapel Hill a laid-back, relaxed, country attitude that mixed well with the team. "Nobody's the same on that team, any year," he explains. "Sure, you may have some kids with the same background, but everyone's different.

We were alike in a lot of ways, but we were different people, different personalities. We had that one goal and that was to be as good as we could be. That carried down from top to bottom."

First or second off the bench was the usual calling for Jim in the 1982 season. He admits more playing time would have been nice, but he was happy with his role.

"If I'm going to play one minute, I'm going to play one minute hard. If I have to play 10 minutes, I'm going to play as hard as I can. I was happy to be a part of that team. Sure, anybody would have liked to play more, but I was satisfied with my role, and Coach was aware of that. I was willing to do whatever was asked."

And finally, the season after the national championship, Jim was asked to do more of what he did best: shoot. Long-range shooting was always Jim's specialty, but now he and the team would get an extra point for his efforts. The three-point circle, adopted by the ACC that season, made Jim a scoring threat, a leader, a hero.

"Eighty-three was a great year," he says. "I wish we had played all our games under the 3-point (rule). It probably would have made a difference in my playing time the first three years. The game totally changed. It made people like me more important. It was good for the game and good for me. I really feel fortunate that I got to play at least a year under the 3-point line." →

Jim Braddock watches the action on the court with teammates Chris Brust, Jeb Barlow (hidden), Michael Jordan and Lynwood Robinson.

But Jim didn't stop there. He parlayed the success of his senior year into a foreign professional career. With stops in Holland, Germany, Ecuador, and New Zealand, Jim kept his reputation intact as a long-range shooter.

Carolina teammate Chris Brust played with him in Ecuador. "He was great," Chris says. "One night, I think he had 57 (points), some real bizarre number. I would just come down and pick for him and let him shoot, because he could shoot the lights out. It was a great time playing with him."

But as happens with many American players in foreign leagues, Jim tired of basketball. "I was kind of burned out from the travel and playing," he admits.

He also felt he was ready to move on to the next level, coaching. He worked with junior players at every stop while playing professionally.

"What I got out of it was playing basketball, getting paid, and getting experience to coach. I ran my own camps and coached juniors. It was a good release to run my own practice, and to put my own thoughts, from what I had learned from all my coaches, into

work. I was getting to see my ideas on the court."

Jim brought these ideas and experiences back to the United States. A business opportunity led him to Jacksonville, Florida, but he says, he knew his future was in some level of coaching. And it was in Jacksonville that he finally put his athletic knowledge to work.

An opportunity to coach at a private junior high school was just the ticket Jim needed.

"I'm kind of my own boss in an athletic department," he says. "I'm primarily the basketball and baseball coach, and I help coach soccer."

Although he is happy where he is, he hopes more opportunities are on the horizon. He became certified to teach tennis while in New Zealand, and now tennis has taken over where basketball left off.

"It's a main hobby of mine now," he says. "Basketball is great, but it's tough to go and find people to play basketball. I love to exercise and the way I do it is go out and hit a few tennis balls."

And if Jim has his way, he hopes to turn his hobby into his profession. In addition to his high school   ➜

Braddock cuts down the net after the NCAA East Regional championship game in 1982.

coaching, he is the strength and conditioning coach for the men's and women's tennis teams at Jacksonville University. Also, he and a partner hope to buy an athletic club someday, with the main focus on tennis.

"Tennis is definitely big here," he explains, "but there's no place in Jacksonville that emphasizes junior development. We've have been talking to the Florida Tennis Association, and it looks like we can be sponsored by them. They can allocate so much money to starting this program, to give scholarships to kids that can't afford to pay. That's what I would really like to do."

Jim is ready to do whatever is needed to make his dream succeed. Just as he did in college. He knows expectations can become realities. He knows it will take sacrifices, just as it did to win the national championship.

He remembers a special moment. A moment only he and his teammates could know. It was after the on-court festivities had ended in New Orleans, and the team had returned to the locker room. "By the time we had got back in there, we whooped and hollered for about two more minutes, and then, it was just silent," he says quietly.

"I started crying. I was looking throughout the room, and just looking at every person that was a part of that team, just looking at their faces, seeing how happy they were, and what it meant to them. Just seeing all those faces and all those reactions – seeing everybody sit back and absorb it. The thought over me was the greatest feeling I've ever had. Being a part of people wanting something as bad as I wanted it, and knowing how to do it, and just doing it. That takes sacrifice.

"Another feeling that was going through me in the dressing room after we won it was just how much I cared and how much I loved every one of the people that was with me. Love takes a lot of different shapes and forms, but it was at its peak after that. We did love one another. As the years go by, you realize it more. It was a great feeling ... nothing like it." ■

John Brownlee

"I just think about not so much that year and the winning... obviously that was a great experience. I just really enjoyed all the guys on the team. I was proud to say I played with those guys. They were the best."

Hometown: Fort Worth, Texas
Height: 6-10
Weight: 215
Class: Freshman

John Brownlee, a Texan born and bred, arrived in Chapel Hill wearing custom-made cowboy boots with Carolina blue leather and Tar Heels on the side.

"It was really exciting to think about going somewhere where basketball was a big sport, as opposed to Texas, where it's kind of a secondary sport," he says.

But after two years, John decided to leave Carolina and return to Texas.

"Everyone's got an ego, and they think they should be playing," he says. "I just really wanted to

JOHN WORE number 32 at Carolina. He wanted to wear the same number at Texas, but he ended up with 55. His teammates called him 'The Speed Limit,' an appropriate name for someone on the move as fast as John was.

play. Although as much as I liked it there, and liked being on the team, that became a very important factor. I knew that I wasn't going to play significantly at Carolina, unless some bad things happened to other people, in terms of injuries. Things you don't want to happen."

What John did want to happen was an opportunity to play. He found that at the University of Texas.

The reason he left Texas for North Carolina became the reason he returned. In a place where basketball was secondary, he had a better chance to play.

"In North Carolina, it wasn't, 'Do you play basketball?' it was 'Where do you play?' " he explains. "In Texas, it was just, 'Do you play?' It was a different mindset altogether."

But it wasn't a different mindset to John. He brought with him from Carolina a winning attitude. Basketball was not secondary to him. "It would have been great to have played more when I was there," he says. "I don't know of a better program, and that's the truth. They do things the right way. I learned a lot from being around that.

"I'm proud to have been associated with the program. I got more than I could ask for out of it, but when I transferred to Texas, things worked out well for me. I feel like I'm one of the lucky ones. A lot of guys, it never works out right for them. I won an NCAA championship, I transferred and won a Southwest Conference championship. I was Southwest Conference Player of the Year."

Wait a minute. Southwest Conference Player of the Year. John Brownlee? Sat on the bench at Carolina? Now a Texas star?

"I didn't really look at it that way, in terms of I'm the star now and I'm going to do this," he says. "We had a good team and played to the best of our ability, and it was just a lot of fun. I knew that I was a good player, and I knew I was one of the best in the conference. It was the right place at the right time." →

John Brownlee played two seasons at North Carolina, then transferred to the University of Texas, where he was named Southwest Conference Player of the Year in 1985. *Texas photo courtesy of the University of Texas Sports Information Office.*

John wore number 32 at Carolina. He wanted to wear the same number at Texas, but he ended up with 55. His teammates called him "The Speed Limit," an appropriate name for someone on the move as fast as John was.

He was drafted by the Los Angeles Clippers after his senior year, but didn't make the team. The Clippers were looking for immediate help, not rookies. That was OK by John. He was looking for immediacy also.

"I really felt, for me personally, Europe would be a lot more fun," he says, "for the fact that you do play and for the experience of doing something different that I wouldn't be able to do otherwise."

Playing in France and Belgium, John felt that his success on the court wasn't being equaled off the court. "You practice twice a day, so you're busy, but I was kind of bored because I was thinking about what I was going to do when I got through playing," he admits.

He reluctantly coached a team of seven- and eight-year-olds to pass the time, but soon found this job to be more than he expected.

"I had more fun doing that, got more out of that, than anything I've ever done," he says.

John's wife, Jennifer, agrees. "He was great," she says, "those kids were just adoring him. They won every game and they worshipped him."

"That's one of my best memories in basketball," John says.

Also one of his last. He decided he had had enough.

"It just came to a point that I was playing ball really hard for five years in college, two years in Europe, and really hard for a year or two before that in high school," he says. "I said, 'Man, it's time to do something else.' "

John is back in Texas now, and real estate is his game. His Carolina cowboy boots are in his closet. "They don't even fit," he laughs. "A couple of sizes too small. I've grown a little bit since then."

Grown in more ways than one, he acknowledges.

"I feel very lucky to have done what I've done, accomplished what I've accomplished. But I think I got out at the right time, because I had done everything I wanted to do.

"I've learned that you've got to keep striving to push ahead. You can't rest on your laurels. It helps me to know that if you work hard and work smart, good things will eventually come. At least that's what I'm hoping. I'm not working to be mediocre." ∎

48

Chris Brust

"I heard someone say, 'Hey, nice foul shot!' I just said, 'Yeah, if I didn't make that foul shot, we'd still be in New Orleans – in overtime.' "

Hometown: Babylon, N.Y.
Height: 6-9
Weight: 231
Class: Senior

Chris Brust scored one point in Carolina's victory over Georgetown in the national championship game. Says so right in the boxscore. The Tar Heels won that game, 63-62. Chris likes to believe the one point difference was his foul shot. At least that's what he told a crowd of 25,000 screaming fans at Kenan Stadium, the day the Tar Heels returned to Chapel Hill after winning the championship.

"Everybody was getting up and saying something," Chris remembers, "and when I got up, I heard,

---

THERE WAS a time when Chris wondered if he ever would be at the right place at the right time. He came to Chapel Hill packing a cast on his broken foot. Carolina was the right place, but the injury couldn't have come at a worse time.

'Hey, nice foul shot!' I just talked as if I was answering him. Everybody got a big kick out of that."

Chris soon discovered his new-found speaking career was not his only claim to fame. Two days later, *Sports Illustrated* hit the stands. On the cover, James Worthy was dunking. Also in the photo, right below James, Chris could clearly be seen.

"I said 'Big deal!' " he recalls with a laugh. "You see the back of my head, my number and my name, I guess you can't beat that. Coach Smith said it's not every day a guy gets on the cover of *Sports Illustrated*.

I just happened to be at the right place at the right time."

There was a time when Chris wondered if he ever would be at the right place at the right time. He came to Chapel Hill packing a cast on his broken foot. Carolina was the right place, but the injury couldn't have come at a worse time.

"That immediately put me a year to a year and a half behind everybody," he says. "You don't want to be sitting there watching everybody else go running up and down. That was really hard."

Corrective surgery and rehabilitation followed. It was a long, slow process.

He began a comeback in his junior year. He didn't play much, but when he did, nice words were written about his efforts, calling him unselfish, a team player, a leader, lauding his perseverance.

By 1982, his senior year, the time seemed right for Chris to show what he could do. He came off the bench to relieve Worthy and Sam Perkins and continued to do the little things that earned him playing time. He had excellent games, but he remembers them more for the victories than his individual play. "It's not a necessity for me to say, 'Gee, I scored 10 points or 11 points,' " he says. "Who cares? If we won, we won. That's what counts."

Chris continued to play after college. A successful season in Holland, where he led the league in ➔

field goal percentage, was his first taste of professional basketball.

"When you go to another country, and you can't understand what they're saying, you're really by yourself," he says. "It was difficult. The experience itself was great because they play more of a physical game and that was really geared for the way I play. One game, our coaches said I should have shot the ball more. That was the highest scoring game I had over there, like 35. He was mad at me. I said, 'I'll think about that.' "

Chris thought about it, and decided to play in South America with former Tar Heel teammate Jim Braddock.

"Ecuador was a true, third world country," he recalls. "Kids were walking down the streets with rifles. We went through the season undefeated. We just kind of finished up there and got out as fast as we could. I didn't feel comfortable there at all."

He was even more uncomfortable when he tried out for the Contintenal Basketball Association team in Puerto Rico. It left a bad taste, he says, so bad that he decided to quit basketball.

"At that point I decided it was just too much like business," he says. "Guys were arguing on the court. No one passed the ball...."

After living in Florida and working with his brother for five years, Chris, his wife, Mim, and their son, Nicholas, moved back to Chapel Hill. The perseverance that Chris had shown during his basketball career began to drive him again. This time, however, it wasn't to succeed on the court, but in the classroom, to get his degree.

Chris was one of a handful of players under Coach Smith who didn't graduate, and he didn't like having that distinction. All the other '82 team members received their diplomas. Chris became determined to get his, too.

"I didn't want to be one of those four or five guys that never graduated," he admits. "I didn't want to be on that list."

He found college a lot easier at age 28. "I got my best grades," he says. "I got an 'A' in math, and I'm a math illiterate. The chance to come back and graduate was probably one of the best things that I ever got a chance to do."

Having graduated in 1988, Chris now works in the Carolina Athletic Office, spending time in each department, gaining experience and insight for a career in athletic administration.

Chris Brust, right, cheers on North Carolina. With Brust are Cecil Exum, far left, and Jeb Barlow, center.

A boxscore doesn't reveal the little things that helped Carolina win the national championship. However, it does have a column for points. Beside Chris' name, the number "1" appears.

A converted free throw, the winning margin.

The shutter clicks. A picture appears on the cover of *Sports Illustrated.*

A class taken. A class passed. Graduation.

The right place at the right time. ■

50

Cecil Exum

"Most people (in Australia) know that I was on the 1982 championship team, and that I played with great guys like Jordan, Sam and James. That's probably going to be the biggest memory that stays with me, playing with those guys and being coached by Dean Smith."

Hometown: Dudley, N.C.
Height: 6-6
Weight: 206
Class: Sophomore

It's a long way from Dudley, North Carolina, to Melbourne, Australia. But when Cecil Exum left his hometown in 1986, "Down Under" was his destination. Basketball was the reason.

When Cecil answers the phone, the stateside caller hears a strange sound, an accent that is half Eastern North Carolina, half Australian. Cecil doesn't say, "G'day mate," or "Let me put some shrimp on the barbee," or anything like that, but the Australian accent is definitely there.

THOSE WHO know Cecil, especially some of his former Carolina teammates, would not be surprised at his popularity in Australia. His Carolina teammates voted him the Most Inspirational Player Award for three straight years.

"I think it's kind of a compliment," he says, when the accent is noted. "When I was with Carolina, the Southern drawl wasn't anything noticeable. I'm used to a different accent now. It's even funny when I talk to my family. I can pick up on that Southern drawl."

Accent or not, make no mistake about it, Cecil has become an Australian, literally. "I'm naturalized, so I hold American citizenship and Australian citizenship," he explains. So much the better, because he is one of Australia's most popular citizens.

"Yeah, very popular," he admits.

In fact, Cecil is to Australian basketball what Michael Jordan is to American basketball, in terms of popularity. He doesn't have high flying dunks, or score 30 points a game, but he does have the charisma and charm that have made him a success off the court.

"I was junior development director with the club I played for," he says. "I went around to schools and did promotional and clinic work. This was a big hit with all the kids, so that made me popular in the basketball community here."

"It's great, and I'm happy for him," Jordan says of his former teammate. "But it is a little surprising. He's always been a little shy."

But, Exum says, popularity and star status are just not the same thing in Australia.

"Being a star here is not like in the States," Cecil explains. "You walk the streets and people recognize you, but they don't approach you like in the States. They don't run up and have that same craziness that they do in the States. Probably, even if Michael walked down the street here in Australia, he wouldn't get mobbed. So I don't consider myself a star."

Cecil may not consider himself a star, but a visitor arriving in Australia might feel differently. A Cecil Exum billboard could stare down at him. Open a magazine, and Cecil could be hawking computers. Or clothes. Turn on the TV, and if Cecil's commercials aren't evidence that he is a star, then listen to this: ➜

Cecil Exum is a popular basketball star in Australia. *Photo courtesy of Cecil Exum.*

Kareem Abdul-Jabbar came to do a basketball tour of Australia after his retirement. "On one side of the program was Kareem," Cecil says. "On the other side was myself. Dudley Bradley toured with Kareem, and he said, 'Looks like you own a piece of Australia!' I said, 'No, not really.' It's just the way the team is promoting me over here. He saw me as being big here."

Those who know Cecil, especially some of his former Carolina teammates, would not be surprised at his popularity. His Carolina teammates voted him the Most Inspirational Player Award for three straight years.

"I think that's the personal achievement that sticks out in my mind the most," he says. "I've always been giving of myself to the team. I tried to be everybody's friend, someone that they could talk to."

Sam Perkins thinks it went beyond that. "Cecil was always the player who was doing something funny, even though he didn't say much. When we went through a rough time, he was always there to lighten it up and take the load off, kind of make everything back to normal. It's always important to have someone like that."

Although Cecil is on the other side of the →

52

world, he has not forgotten how he got there, what he learned at Carolina, how it all began.

"Basketball-wise, even now I find I should be more selfish and more offensive minded. But Carolina taught me a team concept and it's hard for me to break that. I go out and try to think offensive, but sometimes I still go back to the team concept.

"Personally, it's where I grew up. It brought me out of that naive situation that I was in when I was a high school kid. I was just a small-town country boy. It seemed like every weekend (in college), I found myself going back home, just to get away, to get away from school again, until I got used to the guys and the school, until I fit in."

His feelings were the same when he moved to Australia.

"I was apprehensive about this country and about the people. But once I got here and got to know everybody, they made me feel at home. They would go out of their way to do things for you."

Cecil knows that he fits in now. Australia likes him, and he likes Australia. He likes it so much, in fact, that he and his wife, Desiree, may spend the rest of their lives there. "I hate to look at it that way, forever," he says. "But it's hard to get on a plane and go home. That's the only thing I don't like about living in Australia. I can't go back when I want to go back. But I really like it here. If I was guaranteed a trip to the States once every two years, I could live here...."

Still, Cecil acknowledges that home is where the heart is, and he still has a special place in his heart for North Carolina. He finds himself missing family occasions in Dudley – Christmas, parents' birthdays.

"To be so far away from home and to be so far away from family, this place has to be some kind of special," he says. "But I've grown with each situation. I've never forgotten who I am and where I've come from. I think those are the important values to hold on to. I've kept them close with me." ■

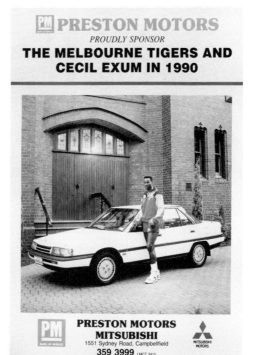

Like his former teammate Michael Jordan, Cecil Exum does commercial endorsements for products ranging from computers and fax machines to automobiles.
Photos courtesy of Cecil Exum .

Timo Makkonen

"The minute we won, I looked over and saw these two guys skyrocket. Chris Brust and Jeb Barlow jumped up from their seats when we won. It was like leaping lizards. Those guys took off."

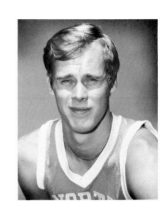

Hometown: Lahti, Finland
Height: 6-11 1/2
Weight: 202
Class: Sophomore

Not often does a basketball player realize and accept that his role is to make his teammates better. Meet one who did.

"I kind of saw my role as giving the starting five the best practice they could possibly have," recalls Timo Makkonen. "I realized I was playing with the best guys in the world, so my chances of having a significant amount of playing time were almost non-existent. Whether you played five minutes versus 10 minutes really doesn't matter anymore. You're part of the

---

HOME IS now Chicago where he lives with his wife Mary and works just down the street from where his former teammate, Michael Jordan, works. But Jordan, of course, is still in basketball and Timo is in hotel management.

---

group that will always be there. When you see the championship picture of the team, there's my name, so I'll always be a part of it."

Timo had the chance to play. But he would have had to leave UNC. He had offers from other schools.

"Coach Smith asked me if I wanted to transfer," he says. "I said I wanted to stay, this is the best there is. I know what my role is here, and I'm happy as it is. I'm getting an education with it, so this is what I want."

"Peek!" Timo would yell during practice. Actually he was saying "pick," but with his Finnish accent, "peek'"was what everyone heard.

"Coach Smith said, 'What is peek?' " Timo recalls with a laugh. It wasn't long before everyone on the team knew what a Timo "peek" was. He went on to become famous for the picks he set in practice, as well as for his swinging elbows.

"The Finnish Flash," says Matt Doherty. "Timo was all bones wrapped up in skin," he says. "He would hurt you in practice. All those Europeans loved to throw those elbows."

"I got a few back," responds Timo, laughing. "It was give and take. It wasn't one-sided, believe me."

"He worked hard," continues Doherty. "He was a very bright, streetwise kid. I think people didn't see that, because they saw this big Finn who had an accent. But he was sharp as a tack. He was good for the team. He kept everybody loose."

Timo kept loose by walking down Franklin Street to his favorite video arcade. "Pop in a quarter and you have five minutes of fun," he recalls.

Today he has a computer at home loaded with his own games. He doesn't miss the arcade games or basketball anymore. He did play in a city league when he lived in New Orleans, but no more.

Now, home is Chicago, where he lives with his wife Mary and works just down the street from where his former teammate, Michael Jordan, works. But Jordan, of course, is still in basketball and Timo is →

Timo Makkonen in action against the Furman Paladins.

in hotel management. Basketball, he say, is "over and done with."

While his playing days may be over, being seven feet tall and not on a basketball court causes him to have to answer a lot of questions. "In a large crowd, you really stick out," he says. "You take it with a grain of salt. Maybe twice a week, somebody asks me how tall I am. They look at you funny at first and then you know what they are going to ask. I can almost tell them before they ask."

Some may wonder why a seven-foot man would not want to continue playing a sport his body was tailor-made for. He could have easily returned to Finland and played with the Finnish National Team, as he had done during summers before.

"If I would have wanted to play in Europe I could have done it," he says. "It was like going back home, and I never really had a desire to go back. That was one reason. The second reason, I didn't want to go to the army. That played a big part of it."

Though he no longer plays basketball, Timo still believes in one of the traits that made him one of the most popular players on the team – teamwork. "It's like something that's part personality, I guess," he says. "It's part of your life. It's like the working world. You've got to get along with the people you work with. It's teamwork wherever you go. That's the only way you're going to succeed." ■

55

Warren Martin

"What amazed me most about that season was our great starting five. It seemed to me that they knew the system so well, and they knew when to go out of the system and on their own. They were all in sync."

Hometown: Axton, Va.
Height: 6-11
Weight: 222
Class: Freshman

Nicknames. They are hard to get rid of once you get one, no matter how old you are. Just ask Warren Martin, or "Cricket," as his former teammates still call him. "It stuck quick," says Warren. "J.B. (Jimmy Black) gave it to me. I don't know where he got it from."

Apparently, there is some controversy over who gets the honors for nicknaming Warren. "I'll take credit for nicknaming him 'Cricket,'" Matt Doherty says. "He looked like the cricket from the Cricket Lighter

---

WARREN MADE good things happen from the first day he stepped on the Carolina campus. He was from a small town in Virginia, and he brought his small town ways with him. Teammates, friends, and fans liked that about him. That was part of the reason he was so popular.

---

commercial. He had this big body and this small head."

Well, no matter who nicknamed him, the name stuck and still follows him.

Nowadays, Warren spends his time as a high school history teacher and an assistant basketball coach at Lee County High School in Sanford, N.C. "What's really strange is to see some of my high school kids come up and say, 'Did they used to call you Cricket?' Where did they hear that from?" he says with a laugh.

The kids probably heard the name during Warren's five years at Carolina. He was one of the most popular players on the team, and fans cheered whenever he entered the game. "That was an adrenaline push ... a confidence builder," he says. "I think they really helped me have a lot more of an impact when I did come into a game. It's something that doesn't happen too often, when you come in and you have a whole building yelling and screaming for you. I was just trying to make something good happen in a few minutes."

Actually, Warren made good things happen from the first day he stepped on the Carolina campus. He was from a small town in Virginia, and he brought his small town ways with him. Teammates, friends, and fans liked that about him. That was part of the reason he was so popular.

Popularity aside, he says that first year was a whirlwind. The winning. The traveling. "We won everywhere, we went everywhere," he says. "The farthest I had ever been was probably Greensboro. From Virginia to North Carolina. Big deal. The next thing I know, we are going out to California."

And wherever Warren and the team traveled, two things were bound to be close: his comic books and his best friend, teammate Timo Makkonen. "He was the older brother I never had," Warren says of Makkonen. "It was interesting to learn from him, and his way of thinking." →

Warren Martin makes his point, reacting to action on the court.

And Makkonen's way of thinking included many trips to the video arcade. "That was something Timo and I really enjoyed. It was a nice break from other things going on. When we were down in New Orleans, one of the first things we did ... we were walking down Bourbon Street, and we ended up in a video arcade."

No, Warren's students probably won't find him in their local arcades these days, but he still likes his comic books. He remains young in many ways, and he likes how that affects his relationships with his students. "I can see where these kids are coming from," he says. "They still see me as that tall guy that played at North Carolina. We're perceived as being North Carolina basketball players. We're nice, polite, and friendly. But that can work against you, when it comes to disciplining the classroom, because that's the way they are used to seeing us."

Although Warren's basketball playing days are behind him, some of his students still ask for his autograph. And he obliges. "My attitude on autographs is, it won't be too long now before they stop asking," he admits. "If they want it I'll give it to them." The requests usually come when he's in the gym, coaching basketball. He doesn't mind then, because he's in the right surroundings. "They really do a decent job of separating the two," he explains. "When I'm in the classroom, I'm the teacher. When I'm in the gym, I'm the coach."

If not for various foot and knee injuries that plagued his career, Warren could be playing today, instead of coaching. He played in Europe, and almost made the squad of the San Antonio Spurs. But he was pushing his body until he could push it no more. "The reason I decided to give it up ... I was just hurting   →

Warren Martin now teaches history at Lee County High School in Sanford, N.C. *Photo courtesy of Lee County High School.*

too much," he says. "It wasn't worth the effort. The training ... the hard work ... and then have something ache and hurt all the time. It just wasn't worth it. To know I'm just tearing myself up and not going to get anyplace."

But Warren did get somewhere, although there were those who had their doubts. "I've always wanted to reach a little bit farther than people thought I could reach," he says. "I had people in high school that said I couldn't make the varsity. When I came out of high school, I remember, I had a few people say I couldn't play in the ACC. They were wrong."

Doherty remembers another story. "He caught

the ball against North Carolina State at home and dunked on Thurl Bailey. He was so happy, his head was going around, smiling to the crowd, and I put my hand up to high-five him, and he missed my hand."

Now, it's his high school players who may miss the high fives their seven-foot tall coach hands out. That's OK. He knows the feeling. ■

Buzz Peterson

"Playing in that final game in the Superdome ... when I first went out there, I got some jitters. If you didn't, your mind wasn't really in it. Once we started playing .. .boy ... it's a game I'll never forget."

Hometown: Asheville, N.C.
Height: 6-3 1/2
Weight: 165
Class: Freshman

Buzz Peterson's childhood dream was to play for Carolina, but if not for a promise he made to his friend and future teammate, Michael Jordan, he may not have become a Tar Heel.

"One night Michael called me and said, 'Hey, remember now, you told me you were going to Carolina,' " he recalls. "And I said, 'I'm not going to let you down, we're going to room together.' The whole time I was thinking, well, let's visit Kentucky. I was impressed with their campus. Then one night I just

---

AFTER AN ATTEMPT at European basketball that was thwarted by broken promises, Buzz returned to the United States determined to stay in basketball. Coach Smith helped steer him into coaching. Stops at Appalachian State and East Tennessee State helped Buzz decide that was what he wanted to do.

---

woke up and said I'm going to Carolina.

"I'm glad I did it. If I had it to do all over again, I would go right back to the same spot. And I kept my word to Michael."

Buzz, who had been a great high school player, highly recruited, went on to have what he describes as an "up and down" career at Carolina. He likes to sum it up this way: "I got my degree, got a national championship, and played under one of the best coaches ever." His freshman year, the year of the championship,

was his best, according to Buzz. He was a key reserve, one of the first off the bench.

A steal and a pass to James Worthy is what most fans remember about Buzz and New Orleans. His face lights up when he tells his version of that game. "I shot the three biggest bricks," he says with a laugh. "The first one, I was going against Pat Ewing, and my mind was saying, 'He's not going to block this shot. I'm just going to throw it as high as I can. He's not going to block it.' I missed the shot, but he didn't block it, so I made an achievement."

But on that steal ... "I've seen some mentions that 'Peterson and Worthy turned the game around.' But before that I just threw the ball away. I just got it stolen from me. They don't show that. They show the steal, and I just flipped it to James, and James went down and made an incredible dunk."

There was a game Buzz did turn around. It was still 1982. Four games after the national championship. But this was a new team, a new season. And no bricks this time. "Twenty-one to 9 at halftime," he says. "I remember that. LSU. People were booing. I remember coming out at the second half and I hit that shot, and hit another one and (Jim) Braddock said, 'Hey, I'm going to get you the ball,' and it started going in."

Buzz went on to hit nine straight field goals, as Carolina came back to beat LSU on national →

television. "We were trying to score the first half, we just couldn't. The thing I remember was Al McGuire saying everybody gets a day in the sun, so I guess that was my day," Buzz says.

The sun still shines for Buzz these days. After an attempt at European basketball that was thwarted by broken promises ("Contracts aren't all they say," he says), Buzz returned to the United States determined to stay in basketball. Coach Smith helped steer him into coaching. Stops at Appalachian State and East Tennessee State helped Buzz decide that was what he wanted to do.

"There's a lot I would like to learn in coaching," he says. "When I was playing, there was something I didn't think about much – the fear of not being able to play anymore. It's something you did all your life, but then, you've got to face reality."

Little did Buzz know what lay ahead for him as a coach. His boss at ETSU, Les Robinson, was about to become the head coach at N.C. State in 1990. "Basically, he was saying, 'We are going to get the job,' " Buzz explains. "I was thinking, is he going to take the whole staff...and then he got the dadgum job, and he said, 'I want you to come down.' At that time, I wasn't thinking about State, Carolina, all that rivalry stuff. It hit me when I walked in the office at N.C. State, and it was like, wait a minute," Buzz says, thumping his head, "how can you do this?"

Buzz called Coach Smith for advice. "He said, 'Before you even get started asking questions, I know what you're going to ask,' " recalls Buzz. " 'You take that job. There's not enough good coaching jobs out there. I look at N.C. State as one of the top 15 programs in the country. You take that job right now.'

"Then he said, 'Have you got anything else to ask me?' " Buzz recalls with a laugh. "Coach Smith told me ... he said, 'Buzz, this is going to be a challenge for you. It's going to be tough the first couple of years, but you're young, you've got a lot of energy. You can do it, and I want to see you face that challenge.' "

Buzz Peterson looks for a pass as he drives toward the basket in a game against Southern Methodist.

It has indeed been a challenge. Not just the coaching, but facing friends and family. "The hard part is handling your old teammates. They're the ones giving me a hard time. They said, 'Traitor!' " Buzz says laughing. His friends, of course, were only kidding. "Braddock called me and Mike (Jordan) called me, and Brad (Daugherty). They all called me traitor. But in the long run they say, 'I'm happy for you. It's a great job for you, and do a fine job.' "

He wore a red sportcoat to the State-Carolina game at Chapel Hill, to quiet State fans who might doubt his loyalty. All part of the job. "My loyalties are to N.C. State," he says. "I'm trying to do the best job I can in bringing in the student athletes to N.C. State and get this program back on track."　　　　→

Like others members of the 1982 team, Peterson is now coaching basketball. A former assistant at East Tennessee State University, he became an assistant at Carolina's archrival, N.C. State, when ETSU coach Les Robinson was hired at N.C. State in 1990.

These loyalties have eliminated any mixed feelings Buzz may have when State plays Carolina, but his family has been a little harder to convince. Although his wife, Jan, supports Buzz and the State team, his parents are still trying to adjust.

Directly in front of his desk in the NCSU Basketball Office is an old State poster of a game against UNC in Reynolds Coliseum. Ironically, Buzz isn't in the picture, but his dad is standing right behind the Carolina bench. "My mom says, 'Do you really want to beat Coach Smith?' and I say, 'Mom, that's a game I really would like to win.' You'd like to beat your old school.'"

And that was exactly what happened in the '90-'91 season, when State beat Carolina 97-91 in Raleigh. "It was like a release that we won that game," Buzz says. "It's off my back and I don't have to worry about it now."

Still, Buzz is grateful for his Carolina connections, and he hasn't forgotten his Tar Heel upbringing. "I'm so happy right now where I am, being able to stay in basketball," he says. "It's like Coach Smith told me, there's not that many good jobs out there in coaching. I've just been fortunate enough, moving up this fast, and playing at Carolina really helped me." ∎

Lynwood Robinson

"I just remember being unbelievably relieved when Mike hit that shot. I remember James going down the court with the ball ... I didn't even see the guy throw the pass, I was so delirious."

Hometown: Mount Olive, N.C.
Height: 6-1
Weight: 176
Class: Freshman

In May of 1984, Lynwood Robinson's family home was destroyed by deadly tornadoes that swept through North Carolina. Lynwood saw the coverage on television, called his mother and got no answer. He jumped in the car, heading for Mount Olive.

"The closer I got to my neighborhood, the worse it got," he says. "Our house was leveled. I saw my dog, Chrissy, but it took me an hour to find my mother. She was at a friend's house, unhurt. I was in shock. My mom grew up in that house. My sister. I did."

LYNWOOD HAS returned to Mount Olive to rebuild his life from the ground up. He works as a disc jockey at a local radio station, gaining experience that he hopes will make it possible for him to move up to a bigger station and town.

After the national championship, Lynwood gave his mother his championship ring. "I gave it to her because it's the only thing I had that I could give my mom to even come close to what's she has given me," he says. "My mom's not rich, but I've never gone without. She got a little misty when I gave it to her."

Lynwood and his mother found her ring among the rubble of their destroyed home, still in the file cabinet she kept it in. It's back in the Robinsons' house, a new home built from the ground up.

And Lynwood has returned to Mount Olive to rebuild his life from the ground up, as well. He works as a disc jockey at a local radio station, gaining experience that he hopes will make it possible for him to move up to a bigger station and town. "You never know what life holds for you, but radio is where I want to be," he says.

Matt Doherty is one of his biggest fans. "He should be on 'Saturday Night Live' " Doherty says. "He could be Arsenio Hall. Lynwood Robinson is a very talented individual."

Not everything goes as planned, even for talented people. Just ask Lynwood. He came to Carolina billed as "the next Phil Ford." Unfortunately, not everyone realized what a toll the knee injury he suffered in high school had taken, both physically and mentally.

"It was my first real test with adversity, which I became a good friend of," remembers Lynwood. "It showed me how fragile things are, and how they can be snatched away from you at any minute. The main thing is how it changed my game. I became a jump shooter rather than a penetrator. It took away a lot of my quickness."

Not only did Lynwood's game change, "psychologically, the fear of hurting it (his knee) again affected me a lot," he says.

The combination of these and other factors led Lynwood to leave Carolina during his sophomore →

Lynwood Robinson transferred to Appalachian State during his sophomore year. After sitting out for one year in accordance with NCAA rules, he started for the Mountaineers all but three games during his two years there. *Photo courtesy of Lynwood Robinson.*

year. "At that time I was really an unhappy person," he recalls. "School wasn't going well...."

He knew that if he transferred, he would have to sit out a year from basketball because of NCAA rules, and he liked that. "The extra year would give me a chance to get myself back together academically...what I was really in school for, to get a degree. Plus, going to a different school, it would give me the chance to play more. To be a happy kid. It's not a good thing to be 19 years old and miserable."

Lynwood says he wanted to grow up a little bit.

He transferred to Appalachian State.

Jimmy Black was one of Lynwood's best friends on the Carolina team. Although he felt like an adoptive father to him at times, Black thought it was best for Lynwood's career if he transferred. "I think he came into a tough situation," Black says. "Everybody on that team wanted to play basketball. If you're not going to play, and that's what you enjoy doing, then you have to make that decision and go somewhere you can play. If that was important to him, then I think he made the right decision."

Going to Appalachian did, indeed, turn out to be the right decision for Lynwood. He started for the Mountaineers all but three games during his two years there. In his first year, he set a season assist record →

63

Robinson works as a disc jockey at a radio station in Mount Olive, N.C. *Photo by Bill Sheffield.*

(since broken), while leading the team in free throw percentage and assists. The next year, as a senior, he again led the team in free throw percentage and assists, as well as steals and turnovers. Not bad for a guy who admitted feeling "rusty" after sitting out that one year.

Lynwood still remembers his last game as if it were yesterday. A loss in the semifinals of the Southern Conference Tournament ended his basketball career. "I was crying like a baby for two hours after it was over," he says, "just realizing that basketball was probably over for me.

"I'm real grateful to the people of Appalachian State. They allowed me to get a degree and play basketball. I gained my confidence and mental toughness back as a player and a person. I think that is not only the key to sports, but also the key to life.

"But first and foremost, I'm a Tar Heel! I can tell you times when I'd go out to my mom's car in the dead of winter and listen to games on the car radio, because the radio in the house had broken," he smiles. "That's

how big Carolina was to me."

Now Lynwood is on the radio. He likes the analogy of a point guard and a disc jockey. Both "run the show." Sometimes things don't go as planned, but this time, he believes, nothing will stop him. With adversity behind him, he is ready to break through with his new career as he did with basketball.

"I can honestly say I've had great enjoyment out of basketball," he says. "It gave me an education. Coach Smith and his staff promised they would do everything possible to see to it that I received my degree. The amazing thing about that was they kept that end of the deal even after I left there. They really stayed on me about finishing school.

"I got a chance to see the world, I got to rub shoulders with some truly, truly great players and make some great friends. I can't ask for anything more." ∎

64

Dean Smith

Q & A

Coach Dean Smith

It was the beginning of summer and Carolina Basketball School. Two and a half months had passed since the 1991 season had ended for Carolina in Indianapolis. From his office in the Student Activities Center that bears his name Dean Smith answered questions about the '82 championship season, as well as other topics.

What single memory stands out from the '82 championship game?

I guess, number one, we were lucky to be there, to get by Houston. My thinking is that you had to be very lucky and very good. It isn't the best four out of seven. Who knows whether we would have won it if it had been four out of seven? But that's the magic of the NCAA Tournament. You don't necessarily get the best team to win the championship. On several occasions the best team hasn't. Fortunately, I think we played extremely well in that game. And Georgetown played extremely well. It has to be one of the finest games, two teams really playing at the top of their games.

Many team members point to the second place finish in '81 and say that if hadn't happened, '82 might have been different. Do you agree?

If we had won in '81, I think it would have been very hard to win in '82. However, if we hadn't been in the Final Four in '81, we might have been just happy to be in the Final Four (in '82).

Some special moments occurred in the locker room after the game. You told the team that millions of people in China didn't even know this game had been played. Why did you take that approach?

To put it in perspective. It's an exciting time, but it's not all of life. It's like "Ship of Fools." I don't know if you've read the book or seen the movie, but Lee Marvin was an ex-ball player, and he said his life was ruined because he couldn't hit a curve ball. Of course, his life shouldn't have been ruined because he couldn't hit a curve ball. He put too much emphasis on being a top-flight baseball player.

The word "relief" comes up often when former players talk about the championship, relief that you and Carolina finally won. Was it a relief to you?

No, I hadn't looked on it in that way. I think there's more pressure to advance each time. To get to the final 8, the final 16....

John Swofford gives the '82 championship credit for helping to raise the money to build the Student Activities Center. Do you agree?

Actually, they had begun prior to '82. Skipper Bowles did a marvelous job raising the funds. That (the championship) may have made it come in $5 million over. That's something I wasn't pushing for. I said to the university, 'There are better ways to spend the money...teaching or somehow working with the School of Social Work or Education.' But as they said, money isn't going to be raised for that, it's going to be raised for this. Then those new people, now their pledge is set up, maybe they'll give to other facets of the university.

You really didn't want the Student Activities Center, affectionately called the Dean Dome, to be named for you, did you?

That was never a goal of mine. I don't think in those terms. It is something that is symbolic, I   →

Dean Smith signals to a player on the court during the 1982 NCAA championship game.

think, and that's the only way it was presented to me. They can't name it after every one of the players who brought this about.

Do you miss Carmichael Auditorium?

We go back and practice when they're using this (the Smith Center) for concerts. It brings back pleasant memories walking in there. It sure does pale in comparison to size. The noise reverberating, even at a practice session, is remarkable, even the chatter on the court, or me yelling. It doesn't do that here.

Many players speak of the rituals with Carolina teams. Let's talk about some of those, begining with upperclassmen rooming with underclassmen. Why do that?

Something I've always believed in that – having the upperclassmen rooming with the younger guys, to kind of learn the ropes. There's something about roommates, even for overnight, sometimes you stay awake and talk more than you would if you weren't rooming together. I think it's good for the team and good for their growth. You have a common denominator of ➔

67

Former North Carolina coach Frank McGuire congratulates Dean Smith after the 1982 NCAA championship game in New Orleans.

trying to be a team, and you learn from one another.

Why do you instill in players "Carolina Time," which is 10 minutes early for everything?

That's just from day one. It's part of the discipline, the punctuality. I guess it's a height of egotism if I say I'll meet you here at 10 and then I keep you waiting 10 minutes. Is my time more important than yours? I'm probably not real great about it if I say that to my wife, that I'm going to meet her somewhere. But I am if I'm going to meet any member of the team. I think it's even part of unifying the group.

Freshmen have responsibilities such as carrying equipment, chasing after loose balls. Is there more to this than giving new players extra duties?

It's kind of a fun thing, you've earned your stripes. I'm not against changing it, but it's funny, every time I bring it up to the seniors, "What do you think we should change?" They don't want to change

anything. They suffered through some of those things, so they want the others to. I think any ritual can be good for unification of the team. We've always had these rituals, like standing up when a guy comes out of a game. I was listening to a sermon by Dr. Anthony Compola, and he was saying tradition builds family unity. I never realized that, but maybe that's what we were doing.

Do you find it hard to control freshman attitudes and egos?

I think most of the young men that choose to come here know what they're getting. I don't mind stars, believe me. I don't mind somebody shooting it if they make a bunch of them. Once we're on the court the freshmen are the same, once we're playing. It's these other things that aren't quite the same. I think we do a pretty good job in not building them up out of proportion.

Michael told me people in Wilmington said "You'll never play there." He said, "I know. I hope   →

I'll start by the time I'm a senior, and I bet I do." He didn't expect to come in and start. In fact, we didn't know we were going to start Michael. We didn't want to start Jimmy Braddock and Jimmy Black against Kansas, because they had a big guard. And Michael really worked hard defensively, I thought unusually so for a freshman. He made the starting lineup as a freshman on his defense. That's what usually keeps a freshman from starting, is his defense.

How to you go about picking players who will mesh on and off the court?

I don't know. We don't really start out doing that. We just try to get good people and hope it works out.

Although all the players' personalities are different, they seem the same after adjusting to their teammates. What causes this?

I don't know whether they become the same personalities, but they do get a common goal. I honestly don't think there is a change in personality. There is maybe a change in attitude towards what's important – the team.

You always go out of your way to make sure the teams get the credit for Carolina's successes, even though the fans and media often want to credit you. How do you handle this?

You've heard me say that I'll take the losses, you guys take the wins, because you're doing what I want you to do. I don't want our players to get attention individually, but through the team goals. I can take the JV's and we're not going to win the ACC. I think the coach-

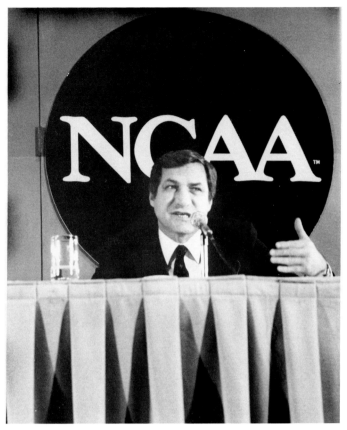

Smith answers questions at a post-game press conference.

DEAN SMITH has been the head coach at North Carolina since the 1961-62 season. Entering the 1991-92 season, he has compiled a 717-209 record, won a national championship, been to the Final Four eight times and won 11 Atlantic Coast Conference Tournament titles.

---

ing staff can create an environment in which they can improve as individuals and as a team. Sometimes you make lucky decisions. Sometimes I've made sound

decisions, like on a last shot, and we get exactly the shot we want and then they miss it. Other times, we goof up and get lucky and score. Our game is such that it isn't quite as set, let's say, as football is.

Many of your former players who have become successful coaches point to you as the source of their success. How do you feel in particular about Eddie Fogler and Roy Williams?

I'm excited for them and Jimmy Black, who's an assistant at Notre Dame. It's funny that most of them turn out to have been point guards. George Karl. Larry Brown. Eddie. I'd like to have them all back. They come back and we sit down and go through a lot of things.

What was going through your mind after losing to Roy Williams' Kansas Jayhawks in the 1991 Final Four?

I thought they did a marvelous job and we were a little impatient. They knew what we were going to do. We knew what they were going to do. If you lose in that situation, I think it's a little easier losing to someone you respect and who is a very close friend, like Roy. →

Smith and Georgetown
coach John Thompson
embrace after the 1982
NCAA championship game.

Why has Coach Bill Guthridge stayed with you all these years, when he had opportunities to run big programs of his own?

The only two jobs I really pushed him to take were Arkansas and Penn State. In fact, he took the job at Penn State. He accepted on the way to play San Francisco in '78. And then after San Francisco beat us, I told him to tell the team so they won't read it in the paper. He couldn't bring himself to do it. He said, 'I don't know what I'm going to do. I'll fly to Chicago and call you.' This is a funny story. He was going to check his bags to Chicago, and then make his decision whether to go to Raleigh or University Station (Pennsylvania). And he called from Chicago and said 'I'm going home. I'm not going to go after another job.' Even though I hope he would take this job when I retire, it's something that he chose. He was happy and he made a good living. He's done a tremendous job. He's the organized one. I'm organized in practice, but he's organized in the office.

Is he almost co-head coach?

Yeah. On the basketball court, I do the talking. I try to delegate. I always want my assistants in my ear. Suggestions. I tell them don't get hurt when I say no. Just give me thoughts. Wherever he would have gone I'm convinced he would have done a great job.

You created many innovations for basketball, but none as popular as the "four corners" offense, which was important in the '82 season. Was that your greatest innovation?

It probably isn't among coaches. Actually a form of that, we did use "4-C" in '82, which was Henry Iba's delay game. We had people like James who could drive out of that, and we had movement with that. We probably used that more as a delay game than we did four corners, although Michael scored an unbelievable shot out of four corners against Georgetown.

Did you feel that the heat you took for the →

70

47-45 Virginia game in the '82 ACC Tournament was warranted?

It takes two to tango, as I said at the time. You'd have to go back to the play-by-play, they hadn't missed a shot. I'm talking about outside shots and we wanted to get them out of their zone, and they chose not to chase, and of course it puts pressure on us too. They had just beaten us at Charlottesville. It isn't like we thought we were a lot better than they were.

That game was the catalyst for the 45-second shot clock. How did you feel being responsible for that?

It was good. I was for the clock and had been. I was blamed for the 3-point shot too. I thought that was the best way to play the game, and if you have a clock you must have a 3-point shot and have it close enough that it doesn't make everybody go to zone.

If we get to the 30-second clock and keep where we have the 3-point shot, I would love it right now.

Let's talk about the players on the '82 team, starting with Jeb Barlow.

Jeb was a walk-on from junior college. He played well, I remember, out in the Cable Car Classic when we went to San Francisco.

OF THE 179 lettermen who played under Dean Smith from 1961 to 1990, 42 of them played in the National Basketball Association, and 31 of them have played overseas or in the Continental Basketball Association. But Smith's players have found success in other careers, too. Fourteen are attorneys, eight are doctors, five are dentists, and 31 are coaches or teachers.

He talks about you coming into the locker room after the national championship game and apologizing to him for not getting him in the game. Why was it important to you to say that to him?

It would have been nice (to get him into the

IN 1976, Dean Smith coached the United States Olympic squad, defeating Yugoslavia in the final game and recapturing the gold medal the U.S. had lost in a controversial game against the Soviet Union in 1972. Bill Guthridge served as an assistant on the Olympic team, while Carolina players Walter Davis, Phil Ford, Mitch Kupchak and Tommy LaGarde were on the squad.

game). You'd like to have a senior in his last game. I think that's always the case.

Jimmy Black, the team leader, coach on the floor. You and he seemed to have a special relationship. Was it?

A great competitor. I had confidence in Jimmy from day one. I think it was good for him when he came here. Dudley Bradley and Mike O'Koren got him hustling a little more, and from then on I was sold on his savvy. We were looking for someone who could get people the ball. I honestly thought because of his defense he would be a pro. But apparently they (the NBA) want guys who can get their own shots. I hear that all the time. It's a different game. The rules are so different.

Did you know he called a team meeting in his dorm room after the loss to Virginia, which many players say motivated them for the rest of the season?

No, and we didn't lose again, did we? I may learn something from this book.

Chris Brust. He came to Carolina injured. Was it frustrating for you to have a player who wasn't able to excel because of injuries?

Not frustrating. He had savvy. We thought he could rebound in this league. Like he said, if he hadn't made that foul shot (in the championship game) ... we needed that one point. He was the one who would go in for James or Sam, and that's a tremendous thing to go in there and not lose ground.   →

71

Smith is rarely at a loss for words on the sidelines.

Jim Braddock. He says he wishes the 3-point line had come sooner, that he could have contributed more. How important was he to the '82 team?

Yeah, in '83 he really played well. But Jim had quickness, too. He was the sub for Jimmy. When Black fouled out in the Virginia game here, Braddock came in and hit some big foul shots. But we didn't use them much together.

James Worthy. Was it tough to see him reach his potential as a college player, then leave for the pros?

I remember sitting with his folks and him in Greensboro. Again, I've said this over and over, every counseling I do is what's best for the individual, and once the season starts, what's best for the team. In my telephone calls, we thought it would be L.A. or San Diego (that would draft him). You had to decide before

the coin flip. That's some gamble. James wanted to stay very much, too. But I thought if you've got a chance to be the first guy picked in the draft, to be financially secure for life ... I said here's the plusses and minuses. It's his decision. I told his dad if I had to choose I would probably say go on, because he can come back and get his degree.

James always seemed so mature to me, even when he came to camp in the 10th grade. He was strong. I thought he was a really great competitor.

Matt Doherty. His name has become synonymous with the term "role player." Was that your intention when you recruited him?

I wish I was that smart to be able to project all this. I can't. Matt was a great passer with savvy, and he had size. I thought he shot the ball well. He had to shoot the ball well, because people were going to give him the shots. →

72

Smith directs his players during a practice prior to the 1991 NCAA Final Four in Indianapolis.

If he shot the ball well – I never want to use the word "unbeatable" in college – but we were awfully good.

Cecil Exum. He was one of the most popular players on the team because of his outgoing personality. Do you think it's important to have a player like that?

I think Cecil was very important to the team. We decided to recruit him after his senior season when he played so well in the state tournament. One-on-one stuff, he'd go by about anybody, like Michael would.

Timo Makkonen. Why did you choose him to be on the team?

He came to camp, and he had potential. He was big and very bright. He came from a different background. Why not have someone like that? He could develop into a fine player. He didn't develop the way we had hoped, but he was very important, I think, to the team. He's done real well. He got his MBA here, and has moved up in the Hyatt Corporation.

Sam Perkins. Critics never thought he was

working hard because of his quiet manner and stoic expressions, but he was one of the hardest working guys on the team. What are your thoughts on Sam?

He was so good defensively. I honestly thought he would be a pro all-star. Now, he was really good early, too. His freshman year, he was starting in the Final Four and he still got better. He was a three-time All-American. He was the fourth pick in the draft. I looked into the draft for him his junior year. Jack McCloskey said he would take him at eight if he was available, that's the best he could do. So I said, "Sam, I don't think you should go pro." And he said, "I hadn't even thought about it." It did work out better.

John Brownlee. He was frustrated at first because he wasn't playing. Is it hard to deal with young players who feel they should play more when you think they still have a lot to learn?

I think John handled it pretty well. You have to or you'll get beat so badly by Perkins and Worthy in practice. I never had a team where it was so easy to pick which guys should start. I told John I wasn't sure he could play at this level, and his dad said, "Maybe you said the wrong thing." It challenged him. He had a ➔

73

great career at Texas. He did do very well and was a third-round draft pick.

Michael Jordan. Did you have any idea how important Michael would become to Carolina and to basketball?

I don't think anybody did. I tell you the one thing that separated him. He improved his speed and his

Still another press conference – this one at the 1991 NCAA Final Four.

jumping ability. He grew two inches between his freshman and sophomore years. Every drill we did, he would listen and go do it. When our drills start out, they're not competitive. Once we have them, they become competitive. Then he had to win the drill. When you put that athleticism with that determination and then that huge competitive heart and savvy, you know he's going to be good. His big jump, though, was

between his freshman and sophomore years. He was winning everything his sophomore year.

He bases the progression of his career on the shot from the '82 game. Is that so?

Yeah, maybe it did something for his confidence, but I think it was his physical maturity. Remember he was a late bloomer. Coach Guthridge said when he was a junior (in high school) he might be able to play in the ACC. But we were the only school looking at him as a junior. Then he came to our camp and was certainly impressive, and Coach Fogler suggested Five Star (camp), and then others saw how good he could be. What's interesting to me, though, at the end of his freshman year to the beginning of his sophomore year, he's not on any pre-season All-American teams. Here he had the good game against Georgetown, and then they say we won't be quite as good because Worthy is leaving. For a guy not even being on any pre-season All-Americans and then being second to the National Player of the Year is really remarkable.

Warren Martin. What did an inexperienced freshman like Warren do to help this team?

He was a special person to be around. He helped James and Sam. He could block their shots. He helped so much in practice that way.

Buzz Peterson. He was rated higher than Michael coming out of high school. What was the difference as Buzz and Michael went through school?

Rated higher by the writers. Michael was higher on our list than Buzz, but we thought Buzz could be a fine player. Of course, he ended up being a sub for Michael and Matt. Buzz was, in the statistical data, right up there in the vertical jump and 40-yard dash their freshman year. But not the next year.

Buzz was a good passer. His knee injury hurt. It hurt his development.   →

Did you ever imagine one of your players would end up coaching at N.C. State?

Actually, as I told him when he called, if you're a history student and they offered you a doctorate of history or to be a history teacher at State – like Willis Casey, their (former) athletic director, he was a Carolina guy, a swimming coach here. I definitely said jump at it.

Assistants, like Jimmy Black, don't bother me as much as the head coach. When Buzz becomes a head coach, or Jimmy, I don't want to play them.

Lynwood Robinson, "the next Phil Ford." It was his dream to play at Carolina, yet he decided to transfer. How do you think that affects a 19-year-old?

That ("the next Phil Ford") was his downfall. I don't make those kind of comparisons. They did have some similarities, like their foul shots. Phil would put it over his head and Lynwood would do it the same way. Lynwood had great defensive potential, and I'm sure he wanted to play more, but Braddock had beaten him out.

I think it was wise (for him to transfer) because he wasn't going to play. It's a growth experience. You should be better off ... We've never really had a player to leave until Clifford Rozier who was probably going to play a lot. If playing is that important, then I encourage that.

How did you feel having Michael, Sam and James playing in the 1991 NBA Finals?

Of course, I watch very carefully. I'm probably more excited when Scott Williams gets in the game because he needs the contract. But that's when I watch pro basketball, when our players are involved. I watch them as much as I can, but I don't watch otherwise.

Which team did you pull for?

I pulled for those four (Jordan, Perkins, Williams and Worthy).

Is it important to have a strong support staff?

I think it's essential to any organization that everybody is with you, and that's what we look for: loyalty. We have four secretaries now and they're very loyal. And certainly the coaching staff I feel very confident with. They're not out second-guessing me. That's a pleasant situation. I can leave and know it's well taken care of.

Whether at the NCAA tournament or at home at North Carolina, it seems Smith is always answering questions at a press conference.

The guys who returned in '83 got to see you fulfill a promise you made at halftime of the Georgetown game, that you and the other coaches would run sprints at the first practice of the next season if they won. Most of the guys laugh hard when they remember that day. What are your recollections?

We stuck to our word. I'm sure it was funny. I'm sure it didn't enter their minds that, "Hey, if we win this, we'll get Coach Smith running the sprint." Jimmy (Black) is probably mad he didn't have the whistle. I guess Braddock got to have the whistle. I'd probably have a heart attack now.

Was it important to keep that promise?

I really believe any leader must do what he says. I think that's extremely important to do what you say.

Players and staffers say they learn to do things right under you. How does it make you feel to →

75

know that you not only are teaching basketball skills but values for life?

People we get, most have gotten it at home. I hope we're trying to take some of the pluses they've gotten from their home life. I think we are lucky that way, that we're getting those people. We're searching for good people to start with.

You and many Carolina players are golfers. Some say that is an escape. Michael Jordan says golf allows him to be normal. Is it an escape for you?

It really is. Escape in that there are no telephones on the golf course. I think it's also fun to be with people you enjoy on the golf course.

You're considered to be not only a coach but a teacher of the game. What has basketball taught you?

I don't know. It's a beautiful game. That's what we are, we're demanding teachers. I think if you look back at your high school or junior high, the teacher you respected is a demanding one. So I think we've been demanding teachers, and caring, I hope. All of the coaching staff. The guys don't believe it some nights, but we really do care.

I think I learn every year. I learn about young people and human nature. Until I get senile, I think I'm a better coach each year.

Finally, after your basketball career is over, how would you like to be remembered?

He gave it a good shot. ∎

Smith talks to players on the bench during the 1985 season.

Assistant Coaches

Bill Guthridge
Eddie Fogler
Roy Williams

Bill Guthridge

Bill Guthridge grabs your thumb and forefinger with his thumb and forefinger and shakes. It's the "handshake of our fraternity," as he calls it, and Carolina players, past and present, have "pressed the flesh" in this manner for many years.

That is just one of the rituals that add to the flavor of Guthridge's personality. Another is his sense of humor. Often characterized as a dry wit, Guthridge sees this trait as more than that, especially with the team. "I like to needle the players a little bit from time to time," he says. "It's one of my ways I interact with people. I don't know where I got it. I enjoy life and being around them and like to kid them. Sometimes in kidding you can get over some points with them that way."

Listen to Buzz Peterson about this approach. "That's one man I really admire," Peterson says. "To some people he may be hard to understand, but I think the world of him. Going through Carolina, I had the utmost respect for him and he's got a little sense of humor that really tickles me. I tell you what, if you're on Coach Guthridge's good side, he'll do anything in the world for you, anything. The players come first.

TEN YEARS ago, the goal was to win a national championship. Ten years later, Guthridge says his goal is to remain the assistant basketball coach at Carolina.

Coach Smith is very fortunate to have a person like Coach Guthridge. He's one of the main reasons that program is so successful."

Like his boss, Dean Smith, Guthridge prefers to give credit for Carolina's success to the players. "It's certainly not that we are magicians, that we've made great people out of nothing," he explains. "We get really good people to begin with. That's one of the really nice things about this job and this university, is that we attract good people. It's fun to work with them, and we are proud of what they accomplish."

Guthridge has known for a long time what path his life was going to take. "When I was five years old I wanted to be a coach," he says. "Most five-year-olds don't know that, but it was something I liked and was fortunate enough to do."

But even Guthridge would not know until many years later that his goal would turn out to have the word "assistant" placed in front of "coach." "In the '70's I thought I would like to be a head coach, and had some opportunities," he says, "but decided that what I really wanted to do was be an assistant coach of North Carolina."

One of Guthridge's favorite parts of his job, he says, is the relationships he has with the players. "I think assistant coaches are always pretty close to teams. One of the functions is to interact with them, and all of us interact with the players. We go by the dorm and check on them to see how they're doing in their studies. That's one of our functions. Our only function is to work with the players."

Guthridge considers himself a teacher. "I like teaching basketball," he says. "That's one of the fun parts of it. I think a teacher has to be patient."

Usually patient and quiet, Guthridge also has a →

Bill Guthridge has been an assistant coach at North Carolina for 24 years.

fiery side. "I think my general nature is to be low-key," he says, "but sometimes when I think I really know that I'm right and not able to get over my point, that's when I get my dander up."

In 1982, his dander was up because people constantly were saying Carolina couldn't win the national championship. "We had won more games than anybody, won a lot of things, been to all those Final Fours, but they were saying we couldn't win the big one," he says. "But there were a lot of big ones to get where we were each year. So it was nice, if for nothing else to have people stop saying that. It certainly didn't bother us, except we wanted what was best for the team."

Guthridge also wanted what was best for his fellow assistant coaches, Eddie Fogler and Roy Williams. "I was worried that they would not be able to get a head job because I was recognized as the top assistant," he says. "I was really happy when Eddie did have the opportunity to leave, and then Roy did also. Eddie's success helped Roy. I miss them but I'm real happy for them that they have done such a great job as head coaches, and I knew they would."

But what about the future for Bill Guthridge? Will he become the head coach at Carolina? Will he retire? "I haven't really thought about it," he says. "The question I always get is not about Coach Guthridge, but how long will Coach Smith go on. I think he'll coach

forever. He doesn't have any plans to retire. As he said, when October 15th (first day of practice) rolls along, if you're not excited about it, then you shouldn't be in coaching. We all still get excited about October 15th.

"I thought for years that he would be the type of coach that would retire at probably 70. There aren't many of those. Adolph Rupp. John Wooden. Bear Bryant. Those type of people. I've always thought that he would be one of those because he enjoys coaching. I don't know what else he would do. He would be successful in whatever he would do, but I don't think there's anything he would enjoy doing more. I want to stay here as long as he's here and have the same job. So I guess that would be 10 more years or so."

Ten years ago, the goal was to win a national championship. Ten years later, Guthridge says his goal is to remain the assistant basketball coach at Carolina. But add 10 more years to that. It's the 2001-02 season for the Tar Heels. If Coach Smith retires, will Guthridge step up or step down?

"I don't know what would happen, but if a situation came and I wasn't ready to retire, I'd probably be the head coach, if they would hire me," he says. "There's just a lot of circumstances. I wouldn't mind being the head coach, but that's certainly not my goal. My goal is to be the assistant coach of North Carolina, and have Dean Smith be the head coach." ■

79

Eddie Fogler

Country music is supposedly king in Nashville, but at the rate Eddie Fogler is going, basketball may soon command as much attention as the Grand Ole Opry.

In his first year of coaching at Vanderbilt University in 1989-90, Fogler led the Commodores to the NIT championship. The following year, Vandy was in the NCAA Tournament. The "picking and grinning" was taking place as much on the basketball court as in the studios of "Hee Haw."

A professed rock-and-roller who is apt to be found listening to Bruce Springsteen or the Rolling Stones, Fogler has found a new admiration for country music since moving to Nashville. "I love it," he says. "I saw the Judds last night. They're great."

His quick adaptation to country music is indicative of how Fogler, a fast-talking New York native, lives. "You never try to blueprint your future, where you're going, what course your life will take," he explains. "Just do the best you can where you are."

When Fogler left UNC for his first head coaching job at Wichita State in March of 1986, it was a very quick decision. He didn't even visit the campus.

A PROFESSED rock-and-roller who is apt to be found listening to Bruce Springsteen or the Rolling Stones, Fogler has found a new admiration for country music since moving to Nashville.

"If someone would have told me I'd ever take over the most penalized school in NCAA history at that time, which Wichita State was, I'd say, 'No way,'" he says. "It just kind of happened quickly. I don't know. It was just time to do something different. Probably if I had given it more thought, or even visited before I accepted, I wouldn't have taken it. I'm glad I did. It was a good experience."

He gave the Shockers experiences they wouldn't forget, including the NCAA Tournament his first two years, and the NIT his third year.

In fact, post-season play has been the norm for Fogler. Every college team he has been a member of, player or coach, has played either in the NCAA or the NIT tournament. And every season, his team has had a winning record.

Vanderbilt has only added to the distinction. But he went to Nashville for more than basketball and country music. "Vanderbilt is an outstanding school educationally, and only attracts very good students," he says. "Kids pick here for academics, as much, if not more than for basketball. I want to work with that kind of student athlete and be in that type of university setting where I know they go on to be successful."

Hailed as one of coaching's rising young stars, Fogler is enjoying his own success.

"There are a lot of other guys who do pretty good jobs who haven't had the chance to get the recognition that I've gotten," he says. "A lot of the reason I've gotten the recognition is because I'm a former North Carolina assistant coach. That automatically means some very good things before you even become a very good coach.

"I'm not close to being as smart or as good as →

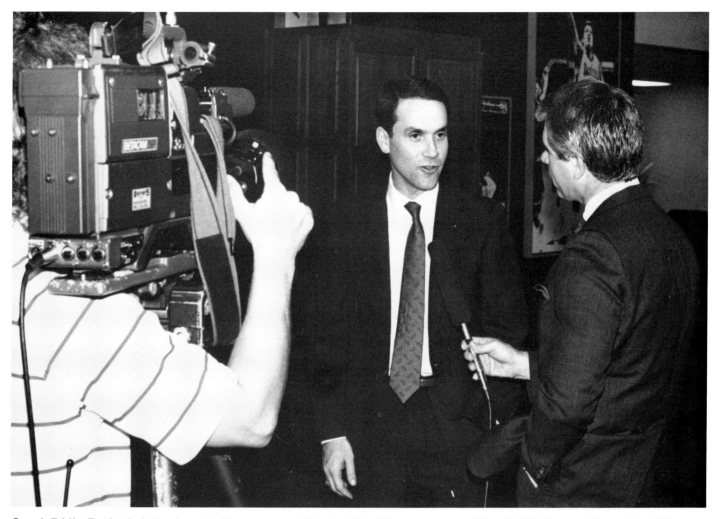

Coach Eddie Fogler is interviewed after a game at Vanderbilt. *Photo courtesy of Vanderbilt Sports Information Office.*

Coach Smith, but I think I was prepared, from an X and O standpoint, to be a head coach. I then got on-the-job training.

"It's like when you get your driver's license. It doesn't mean you know how to drive. When you become a head coach it doesn't mean you all of a sudden know how to coach. You've got to do it by trial and error and make some mistakes."

Fogler tries to learn from his mistakes. "I tell you what, we lost seven in a row my first year here," he says. "We went from 10-2 at one time, to 13-13."

But Vanderbilt went on to win the NIT championship that year, b eating St. Louis in the championship game, 74-72.

Winning that championship, Fogler says, was easier than bringing home the national championship at Carolina in '82.

"Being a head coach is a lot different than being an assistant coach," he says. "Unbelievably different. I felt much more pressure as an assistant coach in '82,

because it was the seventh time to the Final Four.

"A team that was supposed to win it , compared to a team that wasn't even supposed to be there. I was almost so busy in New York (for the NIT championship game), having a lot of people there that I haven't seen in years, that I didn't think about a whole lot, except for preparing the team. In New Orleans, it was really more of a pressure cooker, hoping we could win it.

"It was an unbelievable feeling, something I'll never forget," he says, describing release of pressure that came with winning the '82 championship. "You don't win championships without the last guy on your team being a big part of it. It feels good to be a part of such a great accomplishment. I'll never forget the feeling. I'm still wearing my ring today, yet that's history, and that doesn't help you win games now." ∎

Roy Williams

"Hey, wake up out there!" Kansas Head Coach Roy Williams yells to his players. "Get where you're supposed to be!"

Roy Williams practices what he preaches. He says Kansas is where he is supposed to be. After spending 10 years as a Carolina assistant coach, he decided the time and situation were right to move on. But the move didn't come without hesitation.

"The difficult thing, even when I took the Kansas job," he explains, "was not the decision to take the job. The tough decision was whether or not I could leave North Carolina. I don't think anyone, anywhere has the love for that university and that basketball program that Roy Williams has."

That devotion to Carolina was one of the reasons Williams turned down previous offers from other schools. "The way I tried to look at every one of them" he says, "was just, is this the right job? Does this fit? The first one that actually gave me the feeling that it fit, that deep down inside I'm supposed to say yes to, was Kansas."

And what a good fit it has been. Honor after honor has come Williams' way. National Rookie

fidence in Coach Smith and faith that things were going to work out, because I'm just going to work hard enough to make them work out."

To make things work out, financially, Williams had to take other jobs, such as driving the Carolina football and basketball T.V. show tapes to television stations across the state. "I really needed the money desperately, so I was glad to have that kind of thing," he says with a laugh.

Each Sunday morning he got in his Carolina blue Mustang and took off on a 504-mile, 10-hour jaunt, delivering the tapes. But he took advantage of this time alone. "Those drives really gave me a lot of time to think about basketball and about concepts that Coach Smith was teaching," he says. "Then I would get back and I'd have the J.V. practice and the varsity practice that night. My legs would get tired, but I enjoyed the heck out of that."

Williams frequently uses words such as heck, doggone and gosh, all part of his down-to-earth attitude that made him popular while coaching at Carolina. It's that same attitude that keeps his popularity high in Lawrence, Kansas, where peers and fans often compare his teams and coaching style to Carolina's. It's a comparison he enjoys. →

WILLIAMS FREQUENTLY uses words such as heck, doggone and gosh, all part of his down-to-earth attitude that made him popular while coaching at Carolina.

Coach of the Year in 1988, his first season at Kansas. National Coach of the Year and Big Eight Coach of the Year in 1989. And in his third year, he led the Jayhawks to the 1991 national championship game.

Not bad for a guy who quit his high school coaching position to take a part-time assistant coaching job at Carolina.

"I had given up a very secure situation, with a very secure income, for something that was very chancy," he recalls of that move. "But, I had such con-

"I'm very proud when somebody says, 'Well, you look like Carolina,' " he says. "That's pretty doggoned flattering to me. I think that's the best philosophy, the best style there is, and I think Coach Smith is the best there is, so why should I not copy the best? Particularly when I spent 10 years as an assistant."

But what happens when these two get together? Carolina versus Kansas. Smith versus Williams. The teacher and the student. That question was answered when both coaches returned to the Final Four for the first time since the 1982 championship. The difference was, they were on opposing teams this time.

Coach Williams watched television nervously as Carolina played Temple to gain a spot in the 1991 Final Four. "I was pulling like crazy for them," he laughs. "I still hadn't thought about that's who we would be playing until the game was over with, and I said, 'Phew boy, now that's who you play next.'

"It was a tremendous distraction, because of all the attention that it got. Once we actually got to Indianapolis and were able to practice there, and get in the atmosphere, the whole thing reminded me of how exciting the Final Four can be."

Flashback. 1982. Coaches Smith, Guthridge, Fogler, and Williams all walk out on the New Orleans Superdome floor, in preparation for the game to come. That scene was repeated in 1991, as the Carolina coaches and players took the Hoosierdome floor for practice after Williams' Kansas Jayhawks wrapped up their own practice. Coach Eddie Fogler of Vanderbilt was on the sidelines watching. For a few, brief moments, it was 1982 all over again, except for one thing. "It's the first time I've ever been to a North Carolina practice where they kept practicing and I left," Williams said, laughing.

Some things remained the same, however. Williams and Guthridge still took morning runs together during that stay in Indianapolis – Carolina and Kansas, running together as if things had not changed since 1982. But things *had* changed.

Kansas beat Carolina, 79-73.

"The game really wasn't any different than any other game," says Williams. "I think that goes back to what Coach Smith had taught me, that before the game starts you erase everything, and what you're doing is trying to compete to the best of your ability, to get the team to play as close as possible to its potential, to do the best they can do."

Kansas was the better team that day, even though some of the lustre of that win was taken away by the

Roy Williams makes a point with his trademark whistle as Kansas beats Indiana in an NCAA tournament game. *Photo by Chuck Burton.*

technical fouls called on Smith. "I'm sort of standing there in a daze, but also a helpless feeling," Williams recalled, "because I know right then, number one, Coach Smith didn't deserve that, and I didn't like that he was treated like that, whatsoever. It also bothered me because I knew immediately that would be the big story, instead of Kansas beating North Carolina."

As fate would have it, Duke beating Nevada-Las Vegas ended up being the "big story," and Kansas would lose to Duke in the championship game. Still, Williams, despite all the student-teacher comparisons with Smith, had made his point.

The student clearly had graduated with honors.

"It's not any boy wonder sitting over there on the bench that happens to be a genius," Williams says of his own coaching. "It's those kids who are doing what we ask them to do. That's the reason we're successful.

"You know, I've been lucky, even at the high school level, that I've always had kids that believed in what I was trying to do, and have always played   →

Williams, left, Jim Delaney of the NCAA Basketball Committee and Smith meet prior to the Carolina-Kansas game in the 1991 NCAA Final Four in Indianapolis.

very hard, and been very unselfish. Deep down, kids want to win more than anything. Everybody's going to be selfish to a certain degree, but what you have to do is find that compromise between selfishness and wanting to win, and be able to get those people to sacrifice the correct things, the correct amounts, to be able to win.

"That was the greatest thing about that '82 team. We had some great players in Sam, James, and Michael, but yet, each one of those kids was only interested in one thing, and that's the bottom line, that North Carolina wins."

Now, the bottom line for Williams is that Kansas wins, but he still holds fond memories of that '82 championship and team. "The most vivid memory I have is of the timeout before Michael makes the last shot," he recalls. "All of a sudden, I saw a look on their faces that bothered me. It was the first time that I actually thought, 'Gosh, we could lose.' That thought had never entered my mind.

"Coach Smith was so calm. He said, 'I'd much rather be in our shoes than theirs. We're in the driver's seat. Michael will get it and knock it in. If you miss, don't worry because we've got inside position on the rebounding. We'll get it.' I can remember that talk, during that huddle, like it was last night. When our guys

went back out on the court, they had lost that look of worry and anxiety. Now it was that confident look again. And all of a sudden, I felt better."

Williams is still feeling good about the success of his Kansas teams and his future in that state. His Carolina blue Mustang is long gone. A Lincoln Continental is parked in his driveway now. Instead of driving 504 miles delivering other coaches' shows, he has his own show.

He has been mentioned as the heir apparent when Smith decides to step down, but he dismisses that as gossip. "I've always felt like my life was going to be taken care of," he says, "and I've never been one to sit back and worry about what I was going to be doing next, because I've always been concerned with doing the best job I can, at what I'm doing right then."

After every honor Williams has received, he has gone back and thanked his players for it, sharing it with them. But for those honors, he owes others as well, he says. "Coach Smith, Coach Guthridge, and Eddie Fogler, because what they had given me over that 10 years (at Carolina) is what made me feel so comfortable when I first started at Kansas. It felt good, but I wanted to make sure that the other people who are important to me felt good about it, too." ■

Tar Heels in action

The starting five join for a last-minute huddle before tip-off. *Photo courtesy of the Greensboro News & Record.*

Jimmy Black prepares to shoot a free throw during the semifinal game against Houston.

Matt Doherty drives for a lay-up against Duke.

Even as a freshman, Michael Jordan could soar to the basket.

Sam Perkins looks for an opening against Virginia center Ralph Sampson.

James Worthy scored 28 points in the 1982 championship game against Georgetown.

Buzz Peterson grabs a rebound against ACC rival North Carolina State – a team he would join in 1990 as an assistant coach.

Jim Braddock pushes the ball upcourt.

Sam Perkins gets a congratulatory hug from James Worthy after a Tar Heel victory in 1983. Worthy was visiting from Los Angeles.

Everyone gets in on the team huddle before tip-off.

Michael Jordan gets a hug
from his mother, Deloris.

A family portrait: Michael and his parents. *Photo courtesy of James Jordan.*

94

James Worthy holds his daughter, Sable, while answering questions from the media.

Matt Doherty, right, and his fiance, Kelly, chat with James Jordan prior to a Tar Heel game in the 1990-91 season.

Support Staff

Managers:
 Chuck Duckett
 Ralph Meekins
 David Hart
Trainer:
 Marc Davis

Secretaries:
 Betsy Terrell
 Kay Thomas
 Linda Woods
Athletic Director:
 John Swofford

Managers

Chuck Duckett
Co-head manager
Senior
Class of 1982

"I just remember the feeling right after the game was over. We had accomplished every goal that we had set out to do, and how good it felt. And yet, how hollow you feel as a senior. It's hard to explain. You're so high, and yet it's all over. It's a weird feeling. It's a definite sense of accomplishment, but also a realization for me, that my life was going on to the next step, because my future wasn't in basketball."

Chuck's future is now with a marketing compa-

"THAT YEAR had to be the best managerial staff that I've ever been around. Everyone did what they were supposed to do, and they did it very well. People away from the basketball team can't appreciate this, but even the managers had a role in what we were doing and they were just as important as James, Michael, Sam, Matt, myself, or whoever. I don't think people really grasped that, because, if the managers didn't do what they had to do, then we couldn't be successful in what we were doing."

— Jimmy Black

---

ny, where he serves as vice president. He and his wife, Beth, live in Winston-Salem. Parents of two, they are expecting their third child soon.

Although he used to jump up and down, scream and shout, and liven up the end of the bench, Chuck is more relaxed now. His job and family life keep him busy, but he still finds time for Carolina basketball. He even admits to seeing a little of his old self in the recent crop of Carolina managers.

"I look at them and wonder if I acted as big a fool

as they do, as far as the cheerleading. I know I did. I was the hyper one. I was into it.

"The hardest part of being a manager was being in between, trying to do the right thing for the coaches, but also be the best friends of the players as well. Our job was really to be the middleman.

"It comes up in conversations sometimes, and I say, 'I was a part of that team.' And they say, 'Oh, you played,' and I say, 'No, I was a manager.' To be a manager at Carolina means something that a lot of other places it might not. But it does there, because of all the different jobs and responsibilities we had. There's no question in my mind that I was part of that team." ■

Ralph Meekins
Junior manager
Class of 1983

"It was an honor to be part of the program. It was a difficult job sometimes, because oftentimes you were treated special. Other times you find yourself having to do things that were not as glamorous as you would normally like. But I learned, particularly that one year (1982), how even a manager, if he does the things that he is supposed to be doing, if he does the job, he can make a difference."

Ralph is trying to make a difference practicing law in Raleigh these days. He and his wife Loanne have one son.

Always laughing and joking, Ralph saw his managerial role as being a "connection" for the players. ➜

97

Co-head manager Chuck Duckett, left, cheers on Sam Perkins and James Worthy after the victory over Georgetown.

"We were in a tough spot as managers. We had these great players that were treated like kings on campus, but we had to 'toe the line' and keep them straight. I really did feel like we could treat them as normal as possible. Most of the students didn't. We were kind of the link between the student body and the superb athletes, who were unfortunately put up on a pedestal, and treated differently. We were a link between normalcy and that pedestal. I think that can make a difference.

"We certainly didn't have anything to do when they got out there and started playing. That was their job. But getting them ready psychologically, sometimes being a prankster, just to ease their tension, was something I enjoyed doing." ■

David Hart
Sophomore manager
Class of 1984

"I think the four of us did a super job. I think we were a good complement to the team. We were friends to the players. I don't think you can underestimate how much a team that gets along off the court does better than one that does not. I think the importance we offered as managers was that we kept things running smoothly, and at the same time we fit in."

David is back in his hometown of Asheville these days as an executive banker. He and his wife, Cindy, have a baby on the way.

David was the 23rd member of the Tar Heels, which meant, because of NCAA rules, he did not sit on the bench at the Final Four, nor did he receive a championship watch awarded to team members after the victory over Georgetown.

"When we flew back to Chapel Hill Monday morning, Coach Guthridge said 'Coach Smith wants to see you.' I got there and wasn't expecting anything. He just said, 'I really appreciate what you've done for this team. Your contribution is very real, and I appreciate all the time and work you've put into it, and I'd like for you to have this.' He handed me a box, and I opened it up and it was his national championship watch. I said, 'Coach, you really don't need to do this, I appreciate it, but this is yours.' He kind of laughed and said, 'I've got other watches.' That made such a statement to me about him. Here was his first national championship, and the one tangible piece of evidence he had, he gives it away. It means more to me because of how I got it than if I would have gotten it as part of the awards ceremony. My main feeling was, 'Wow, what a man,' that he would do this. What a genuine man he is." ■

98

Trainer Marc Davis

According to Marc Davis, the 1982 season was easy for him. He had no major injuries or illnesses to deal with, and that was a rare experience. "Not only do you have to be good, but you've got to have a little bit of luck," he says. "We only played seven or eight guys most of the time, and fortunately we didn't get anybody hurt the whole year. Our five starters were real iron men. They played the majority of the minutes the whole year. That was unusual."

Davis is still tending and mending the Carolina basketball players throughout the past decade. He has stayed with his job because, he says, "it fits."

Easy going and popular with the players, he bears the nickname, "Skate," because his flat-footed walk, with his arms behind his back, resembles a skating motion. But it's his "nothing-fazes-me" attitude that many of his '82 teammates remember.

It was more than taping ankles and checking pains, they say. He was a friend and confidant. "He saw that I loved the game, and I didn't want to miss it," Michael Jordan explains. "He really helped me out in that sense. He really stayed in tune with me. I stayed practically injury-free throughout college." ∎

Basketball Secretaries

Betsy Terrell, Kay Thomas, and Linda Woods had the jobs other secretaries could only dream about. Famous athletes and personalities walked through their doors every day. Good seats at basketball games. Exciting trips following the team. What many people don't see, however, is the amount of work these three women performed every season. Running the Carolina Basketball Office was no easy task. A mountain of work met them every day.

Paperwork, organizational work, planning, and telephone calls. Oh yes, the telephone. It rings constantly. Many of the calls are for legitimate basketball reasons, but many are not. Some people want to discuss this or that; others want tickets. Many just want to talk with Coach Smith or a player. It is the secretaries who must field and screen all these calls.

And the lines were flooded after the 1982 championship game.

"The phones always ring, but the main thing I remember was the tremendous amount of fan mail," says Betsy Terrell, administrative secretary in 1982. "It just came from everywhere, not only North Carolina, but all states. A lot of congratulations."

These days, Terrell can either be found on the

Betsy Terrell
Kay Thomas
Linda Woods

---

golf course or with her husband, Simon, the former head of the North Carolina High School Athletic Association. After many years with Carolina Basketball, she chose 1982 to be her last year of full-time work. Little did she know what gratification lay ahead. "Working in the basketball office, and being there for so many years, I think it was just the ultimate, the icing on the cake," she remembers. "We came so close so many times, that it was just a great, great exciting time. It was the culmination of a lot of hard work."

Linda Woods, now executive secretary to Smith also remembers well that final game of 1982. "I was in shock that we had actually won, and then to think that it really was a national championship was more than I could absorb," she says. "It was the longest game I've ever sat through." She has sat through many games in her years at Carolina and hopes to see many more before she leaves the basketball office. "To me, it's →

not just a job, it's a life. It becomes a part of you, and the players are just like your own children."

Kay Thomas has no trouble recalling the national championship game. "I know the meaning of hysterical, because I was," she remembers. "Totally. Crying. Laughing. Screaming. I knew we had it won. I knew it was ours. It had to be ours."

Thomas is close to many Carolina players, past and present. One of her best friends is Jimmy Black. Seeing him on the Superdome floor with his head in his hands, crying, was more than she could take. "It broke my heart. It made me feel good, but was breaking my heart at the same time."

Thomas recalls spending "forever" answering letters after the national championship. "I even had to borrow a typewriter and take one home and work there answering the mail we got," she says. "All of it got answered. Everything."

Thomas is continuing her duties in the basketball office. In addition to her work with the coaches and team, she also plays a big part in organizing the Carolina Basketball School during the summer. She just received her 20-Year Service Pin from the university and she sees no end in sight. Why has she stayed with Carolina so long? "Loyalty," she says. "Getting to

IN ADDITION to her work with the coaches and team, Kay Thomas also plays a big part in organizing the Carolina Basketball School during the summer. She just received her 20-Year Service Pin from the university and she sees no end in sight.

know the guys. I can't imagine not knowing them. You think about leaving and you go 'I won't know them anymore. I won't be a part of it anymore.' "

Some may think that season after season the jobs of the secretaries would become old hat, but not to Thomas and Woods. "It does change," Woods says. "Every year there is the excitement of the moment, and anticipation of what's to come. And then it's over, and you're cleaning up behind yourself, getting stacks of papers sorted, and then all of a sudden you're going again, hard as you can go. Time goes by so fast, you don't even realize that another year has gone." ■

Athletic Director John Swofford

John Swofford

John Swofford is really not a member of the Carolina basketball staff. As athletic director, he is in charge of the basketball program and all other Tar Heel athletic organizations. He says 1982 was a turning point for Carolina athletics. "I was just two years into the job as athletic director," he recalls. "We had actually gone almost 25 years without a national championsip in any sport, since the 1957 basketball championship. We had gotten the lacrosse national championship the spring before, and then the basketball one was the special one, the real plum.

"Basketball at Carolina has always set somewhat of a standard for all of our sports programs, not only competitively, but off the court as well, in terms of the academics and integrity of the program. Winning that national championonship just helped continue setting a very high standard for our programs in every way." ■

Reactions

Former players

The University of North Carolina basketball team continues to turn out quality players who go on to successful careers in the NBA, as well as to jobs as coaches and athletic administrators. In fact, Carolina has been one of the leaders in the number of players on NBA rosters. Many of those players took a keen interest in Carolina's 1982 national championship.

Larry Brown	Rick Fox
Billy Cunningham	Bobby Jones
Brad Daugherty	Mitch Kupchak
Walter Davis	J.R. Reid
Phil Ford	Kenny Smith

Larry Brown, left, and Dean Smith relax after a round of golf.

Larry Brown

Class of '63
Coach of the New Jersey Nets in '82
Now coach of San Antonio Spurs

"The unfortunate thing about national titles is no matter how good you are every year, they only equate one team as being the winner. As many big wins as Coach (Smith) had, as many great teams as he had, they will look at that as his greatest accomplishment, but I don't. I can count a hundred unbelievable accomplishments on the court, and thousands off the court. But I was really proud of him, because the average person looking at it (the championship), now says he is the best." ■

102

Billy Cunningham, center, with North Carolina assistants Roy Williams, left, and Eddie Fogler after the 1981 NCAA championship game in Philadelphia. Cunningham, then the coach of the Philadelphia 76ers, thinks he jinxed the Tar Heels that year.

Billy Cunningham

Class of '65
Coach of the Philadelphia 76ers in '82
Now a partner in the Miami Heat

"I didn't go to New Orleans because I thought I was bad luck. I went to Philadelphia when they lost (in '81), so I decided that I was bad luck and would stay home and watch it on TV. At my house, everyone was watching on different TVs so they could just go crazy or yell at the TV.

"What a great game. You look back on that team ... my goodness, what a basketball team. You put that team in the NBA and you'd win a championship or two, at least." ■

Brad Daugherty

Class of '86
Senior in high school in Black Mountain, N.C. in '82
Now playing for the Cleveland Cavaliers

"No doubt about it, it's one of the major reasons I came there ... that championship game. It was wonderful. It was an awesome feeling coming to that campus, being a part of an NCAA championship. Once you get into that family at North Carolina, you're a part of the future and a part of the past, so it's a great feeling for me." ■

Brad Daugherty, left, joins Michael Jordan and James Worthy on the court during introductions at the 1991 NBA All-Star Game in Charlotte.

Walter Davis

Class of '77
Playing for the Phoenix Suns in '82
Now playing for the Portland Trailblazers

"It was a great feeling that night to win. They sent out bumper stickers, '82 National Champions, so I put one up on my locker. I was just so happy for Coach Smith and all the players and everybody at UNC. It was great to finally win, because he (Smith) deserved to win because he is such a good coach and good person.

"I felt like I was a part of that, too. It's a whole family, everybody can enjoy that and share in it." ■

Phil Ford

Class of '78
Playing for the Kansas City Kings in '82
Now an assistant coach at Carolina

Phil Ford during his playing days
at North Carolina...

"I was very happy for my alma mater and the coaching staff and all the players on the team. They played some exceptional games. I think they were ranked number one before the season started and finished the season number one. That's very hard to do.

"It always brings back memories whenever I see Carolina play. It was the best four years of my life. I was just very happy for those young men. I always feel a part of North Carolina Basketball. I kid Coach Smith and tell him he's the only man I know who has over 180 children and only four of them are girls." ■

...And today at Carolina, where he is now an assistant coach.

Rick Fox

Class of '91
12 years old in Nassau, Bahamas, in '82
Now playing for the Boston Celtics

"I happened to be in a hotel with my father, and I was sitting around in the lobby waiting. There was a game on, a lot of fans, a lot of tourists (were watching). I didn't really understand what was going on, but I remember Carolina was playing Georgetown. There were about 6 or 7 minutes left in the game.

"Obviously, Carolina came out on top, and that kind of left an impression in my mind, and two years later, when I first came to the States, the first thing I told my coach was that I wanted to play for Carolina." ■

Rick Fox scores two for the Tar Heels.

Bobby Jones

Class of '74
Playing with the Philadelphia 76ers in '82
Now athletic director and basketball coach at Charlotte Christian School

"During a game and before a game, I rarely ever get nervous, but watching that game, I really got nervous and very tense about it. As it unfolded, we ended up winning, and it was a great feeling. They had a good team. You worry about, no matter how good a team is, in college ball, strange things happen. You never know what's going to happen. You just hope that your talent will carry you through, and it did.

"I felt a part of it. I think that group is closer, the Carolina players, much, much closer, than any other school." ■

Bobby Jones, right, and Jimmy Black conduct a clinic in Charlotte.

Mitch Kupchak, right, and James Worthy wait to take the floor during the dedication ceremonies at the Dean E. Smith Student Activities Center in 1986.

Mitch Kupchak

Class of '76
Playing with the Los Angeles Lakers in '82
Now assistant general manager of the Los Angeles Lakers

"When I was going to school, looking back on it now, it was never considered a big deal that we had never won a national championship. It was really something the media picked up on. Even if they had not won that thing in '82, it's still the best basketball program in America.

"I think the fact that such a big deal was made about him (Coach Smith) never doing that (winning the national championship), and the fact that he finally did it, I was happy to see him not have to deal with that anymore." ■

J.R. Reid

Class of '90
Eighth-grader in Virginia in '82
Now playing for the Charlotte Hornets

"I wasn't really a big Carolina fan in '82. I was more for UCLA, or maybe even a Georgetown fan. It was a good game for me to watch. I loved the players. Ewing. Worthy. Perkins. It was just a great game to watch." ■

J.R. Reid, now playing with the Charlotte Hornets, defends against Sam Perkins of the L.A. Lakers during the 1991 NBA season.

Kenny Smith

Class of '87
17 years old in New York in '82
Now playing with the Houston Rockets

"I think, overall, that's when everyone's awareness of the school magnified, doubled. Including mine. That's when I saw the system on a level that hadn't been played before and that's when I became interested in going to the school.

"It was one of the best college games ever played. Being a New Yorker, I have to say, I almost was pulling for Georgetown, because it's an 'area' school. I guess fate has it that you always follow a winner, so I went down to Chapel Hill and had a great four years there.

"That game set an intimidation factor almost – just by wearing a Carolina uniform it gave the guys after that, a sense of pride." ■

Kenny Smith, who holds the UNC record for assists, is now playing with the Houston Rockets.

Carolina celebrities

Some of Carolinas's celebrated alumni share their thoughts on the 1982 national championship.

| Charles Kuralt | Alexander Julian |
| Curry Kirkpatrick | Jim Hunt |

Charles Kuralt

Class of '55
Anchor and reporter for CBS News
His nephew, Justin Kuralt, was head manager on the 1991 Carolina team

"I remember that unbelievable last few seconds when the Georgetown kid seemed to pass the ball to Worthy. What I remember is that photograph that somebody took, that showed the scoreboard, and Worthy had just taken the ball, and he's driving down the court, and everybody is standing and looking on. It's one of the greatest sports photographs I've ever seen. The whole story is just told in that magnificent photograph. I don't really have any personal memories; I'm sure it made me feel great.

"The one I remember is the one in '57, that triple overtime. I remember watching that on an old-time black and white television, and jumping so high I hit my head on this low ceiling in a recreation center in Charlotte, where I was watching." ∎

Charles Kuralt is the host of "Sunday Morning" on CBS.

Curry Kirkpatrick, right, and Lesley Visser of CBS Sports during the 1991 NCAA Final Four in Indianapolis.

Curry Kirkpatrick

Class of '65
Senior writer for *Sports Illustrated* and reporter for CBS Sports
Covered the '82 national championship for *Sports Illustrated*

"New Orleans was an exciting time and I loved the game. It was one of the great games. The disappointing thing, from a professional point of view, was that they cut the story that I did maybe by 100 lines, really cut it. A lot of the stuff I wrote about the game and the championship was cut.

"I really didn't have time to reflect on the game until several hours after. It was only after I had filed the story, about 3 in the morning, and going into the French Quarter with some other Carolina people that I was able to enjoy it as a fan and just sit back and say my school just won the national championship.

"A lot of people think I have a lot of 'ins' into the Carolina program, that I get some special deals that *other journalists don't get. Nothing could be farther from the truth, because Dean has always thought that I bend over backwards, too far backwards, in coverage to Carolina and I'm not fair enough to them.*

He's made his feelings known. We put J.R. Reid (a freshman) on the cover one year. He got upset about that. We wanted to put Michael Jordan (freshman) on the cover of that year (1982) with the four other players (starters). He wouldn't let us do that." ■

110

Alexander Julian

Class of '69
Internationally known fashion designer
Currently designing new Carolina basketball uniforms

"First of all, as a kid growing up in Chapel Hill, I remember the '57 championship. Albeit I was only eight years old, it was something that set up the '82 victory in my mind.

"I had been in New York for several years. I gathered as many Tar Heel friends as we could muster and we rented a private screening room that had a big-screen TV. We got barbeque and some cold things to drink and had a party. There at the end, the whole place went nuts. We started partying and celebrating just like we were still students. Somewhere about 3 in the morning, the idea was put forth amongst the 20 or so who were left that the appropriate action would be to travel from Manhattan to East Hampton to watch the sun rise on the first day of the Tar Heels' national championship.

"It sounded like a hot idea and everybody says, 'Yeah, let's go,' and then suddenly it was 3:30 and you find that there's four of you. We took a bottle of Dom Perignon – I think it was an '82, actually – and went out to East Hampton and got there about 6, just before the sun was about to come up. We stuck the bottle in the sand so the waves would chill it for a while and sat on the beach. A giant wave, evidently sent by Georgetown, came and took the damn bottle out to sea and we never saw it again.

"We went back later that afternoon and found car tracks from a fisherman who must have thought he had struck gold finding a bottle of Dom Perignon floating up on the beach.

"There's no finer coach than Dean. We all wanted it for him. We wanted it for the team itself. It's a tribute to him and the hard work of all his players. What I'm looking forward to most is the next national championship, wearing my uniforms. ∎

Alexander Julian, who designed uniforms for the Charlotte Hornets, is designing new uniforms for the North Carolina basketball team. *Photo courtesy of Alexander Julian Enterprises.*

Former North Carolina Governor Jim Hunt shakes hands with Buzz Peterson after the NCAA championship game.

Jim Hunt

Class of '64 (UNC School of Law)
Governor of North Carolina in '82
Represented North Carolina in New Orleans

"It seems like yesterday to me. My heart was in my throat when Jordan took that looong shot. I said to myself, 'How can a freshman make a shot like that?' Little did we know then what we had in Michael Jordan.

"It was one of the greatest thrills of my life to see the Tar Heels win in 1982. It was the first national championship I had ever personally seen, and it seemed like God was on our side. My admiration for Dean Smith and his program is so great that it was just wonderful to see the very best prevail with a national championship that was so deserved.

"I think it gave our state's image a real shot in the arm. I could tell immediately afterwards in recruiting industrial prospects that they had a new recognition of, and appreciation, for North Carolina. They saw us as real winners and the Dean Smith quality approach to coaching and teaching set North Carolina apart from the rest." ■

Almost

1980-81 NORTH CAROLINA BASKETBALL TEAM

The 1981 Team

The 1981 Team

"I always kept thinking about the guys that were on the team the year before, because they really deserved part of this. They were part of the team that gave us the confidence and the know how to get there. I don't think enough's been said about that year's team."

– Jim Braddock

Senior players
Pete Budko
Eric Kenny
Mike Pepper
Al Wood
Senior manager
Lindsay Reed

Pete Budko, Eric Kenny, Mike Pepper, Al Wood, and Manager Lindsay Reed were seniors on the team that lost to Indiana in the national championship game in 1981. It was the day President Reagan was shot. Team members were wearing green ribbons on their uniforms in memory of the child killings in Atlanta. It was a bad day all around.

Time has faded many memories of that game and team. The 1982 national championship helped erase the images of that Monday night in at the Spectrum in Philadelphia. But the memories of the 1982 Tar Heels remain clear about the team that almost claimed the championship the year before they finally got it. Many

---

THE FIVE SENIORS on the 1981 team do not feel cheated by not having been on the championship team. They know that they helped lay the groundwork for the championship season.

---

say that without the experience in 1981, the 1982 championship might not have come out the way it did.

The five seniors on the 1981 team, however, do not feel cheated by not having been on the championship team. They know that they helped lay the groundwork for the championship season. By 1982, they had made a difficult transition moving out of the spotlight as team members to become fans, and were cheering Carolina on all the way.

• • •

Pete Budko and his wife, Pam, live in Charlotte

with their two children. Pete is a bank vice president. Although injuries kept him out for much of the season, Pete still thinks the 1981 experience was a good one, if not for him, certainly for the 1982 team.

"Just to go through the experience and know what to expect," he says. "I think you've got to go there not as 'high' as someone going there for the first time. It's so easy to go into those games so fired up that you kind of lose sight of what you're supposed to be doing. You see a lot, especially as the tournament goes on and on, of people that are so fired up, they burn out after five minutes. I think knowing what to expect, knowing how to handle the media and everything that you're exposed to, it's just got to be the best experience.

"There's a lot to be said for maturity, as well. All those guys were a year older, and had one more season under their belt. They were that much more prepared."

• • •

"That day and a half in between games, just about every hour or so, I pinched myself, and I would talk to somebody on the team, and say, 'Do you really believe we're playing in the national championship game?'" Dr. Eric Kenny remembers.

Currently, Dr. Kenny makes his rounds in Lynchburg, Virginia, where he lives with his wife, Karen, and their daughter. He holds fond memories of that 1981 Final Four, and thinks it set the pace for the coming year.

"You feel a certain contribution, just from what you did as a participant in the previous year," he ➔

Coach Dean Smith with senior Al Wood, center, James Worthy and Jimmy Black prior to the 1981 NCAA championship game in Philadelphia.

says, "just a builder of the program. Mostly, that's a private feeling, but it's there. I'm sure it had to be at least a contributing factor. The disappointment of having almost been there, but not quite. That feeling had been experienced and wasn't anything anyone wanted to repeat, I'm sure."

• • •

"On that night we were beaten by a better team," Mike Pepper says, referring to the loss to Indiana in the 1981 championship game. "We were on a roll. We rolled through the ACC Tournament, and through the Western Regional, and into the Final Four. But as much of a roll that we were on, they were on a bigger roll."

Mike says he's had a long time to think about that loss in 1981 that ended his basketball career. He is back near his hometown of Vienna, Virginia, in neighboring Oakton, with his wife, Lily, and daughter. His career now is in commercial real estate, but often the topic of conversation is his days at Carolina and the '81 and '82 teams.

"In addition to the accomplishments of the '81 →

team, I think you also have to include the accomplishments of the six teams that went to the Final Four before our team," he says. "We were all very aware that Coach Smith had been to the Final Four a number of times, and were familiar with some of those teams. So, I think all of those teams before, also, have to be included, maybe in a small way, in contributing to the championship."

• • •

Al Wood checks the boxscores every year after the semifinal games of the Final Four. He is checking to see if his record of scoring 39 points in a semifinal game has been broken. Each year for 10 years, the answer has been no. The record still stands.

"What a surprise that it is still standing, with the mere fact that they have that 3-point shot," Al says, speaking from his home in France, where he plays professional basketball in a European league. Al, his wife Robin, and their three children also have a home in Monroe, North Carolina, where they return each summer.

From there, Al goes back to Chapel Hill to work out and play basketball, to return to the glory days. "I would have thought that someone would probably have broken it by now with the 3-point shot. I look back and see that no one has broken it, and that's still real special."

He confesses that he has never gone back and watched that '81 game and his 39-point performance. He didn't want to dwell on it, preferring to look toward his professional career.

"When we went in '81, we wanted to win it, but to be honest with ourselves, we were just glad to be there," he admits.

The three previous years had been disappointing to Al and his teammates, who lost in the first round of the NCAA Tournament each year. "So for us to get to that point, it was a great thrill.

> "**WHEN IT** came down to the actual championship game, we all wanted to win it bad. For the seniors, it was a one-shot deal. But it seemed like something was missing. It seemed like we just didn't have what had gotten us to that point.
>
> "And I think for the '82 guys, coming back, they realized that. I think they realized that very much, and they knew that, 'Hey, fellas, this is it, this is a one-shot deal!' That was the attitude they had, to lay it all on the line, because you just don't get this opportunity too often."
>
> **– Al Wood**

"When it came down to the actual championship game, we all wanted to win it bad. For the seniors, it was a one-shot deal. But it seemed like something was missing. It seemed like we just didn't have what had gotten us to that point.

"And I think for the '82 guys, coming back, they realized that. I think they realized that very much, and they knew that, 'Hey, fellas, this is it, this is a one-shot deal!' That was the attitude they had, to lay it all on the line, because you just don't get this opportunity too often."

• • •

Head Manager Lindsay Reed thought the 1981 team was going to win it all. "I thought we were a team of destiny," he says. "It seemed like we were getting the breaks, and we got on a roll."

Lindsay is back in Pennsylvania, an elementary school teacher. He and his wife, Tracey, are parents of three children.

"I wished I was still a manager, for sure," he says. "It was somewhat disappointing not being a manager on the team that year, but the fact that they won it all didn't make it seem so significant that I wasn't.

"It just seemed like from day one, the '82 team was a team on a mission. So many of the players were returning, and to get so close and to taste it ... I think there was really a determination." ■

116

Conclusion

I'm the one who stood under the basketball goal as the 1982 Carolina players went through their warm-ups. As co-head manager of the team, one of my duties was to count each layup and keep track of the misses. If you missed two consecutive layups, or missed one in consecutive games, you would be running in the next practice. It's hard to think that someone could miss one of the easiest shots in basketball, but it did happen.

In New Orleans, at the Superdome, on the night of March 29, 1982, 110 layups were taken by my teammates in the pre-game warmups. Only two were missed. Lynwood Robinson and Sam Perkins were the guilty parties. I reported my tally to Coach Smith before the game began. Jimmy Black or Chris Brust usually asked me who, if anyone, had missed.

I think Coach Smith used this as a barometer of how focused our team was. Were they concentrating? Were they really warming up? Every time someone missed a layup, I usually caught a glance. I guess they

---

TIME HAS blurred my memory over the last 10 years. Many important moments of that great year are now just faded newspaper clippings, photographs, and notes.

---

were checking to see if I had caught them. Was I concentrating?

Yes, I was, but I wish I had been paying closer attention. Time has blurred my memory over the last 10 years. Many important moments of that great year are now just faded newspaper clippings, photographs, and notes.

Putting this book together has been somewhat of a reunion for me and other members of the team. Many of those memories have been rekindled by our conversations. All of us have forgotten some things, but collectively, it seems, nothing is lost. Sure, some stories have different versions, depending on the tellers. That's only natural. But the consensus among all the guys is a great feeling of joy when they talk about that special season.

I could hear it in their voices. I could see it in their eyes. Excitement. Happiness. Satisfaction.

But there was also sadness. Most of us miss seeing each other on a regular basis. Our team was close on and off the court. We were friends as well as teammates. The camaraderie went above and beyond the winning.

While working on this book, I became a relayer of messages and information. "How is Matt doing?" one teammate would ask. Or "Where is Braddock now?" "Is Jeb still in Arkansas?" "The next time you talk to him, tell him I'm going to call him." It would go on and on.

"I remember when...." somebody would say, and we would be off into another story.

There was never a loss for words when talking about the championship and the season that preceded it. "The right place at the right time" was a phrase mentioned by many members of the team, but one word kept coming up with almost everyone.

Relief.

Relief that Coach Smith had finally won "the big one." Relief that "the monkey was off his back." Relief that he could now be called a champion, even though we all knew he always had been that.

My conversations with the players, coaches, trainer and managers reinforced my belief that some things were distinctive about our team.

Nicknames, for one. The team was filled with them. Cricket (Warren Martin), J.B. (Jimmy Black), Stick (James Worthy), MoTi (Timo Makkonen), Perch (Chuck Duckett), Bradrock (Jim Braddock), Skin (Lynwood Robinson), Skate (Marc Davis). They didn't seem important then, but for some reason they do now. Those names are a pleasant reminder of the past, a common bond between teammates. Some of the guys still answer to their nicknames and can tell you the exact moment when they were "christened."   →

David Daly, co-head manager of the 1981-82 North Carolina basketball team, checks the clock during a timeout during the 1982 NCAA Final Four.

A conversation didn't pass without the mention of Warren Martin and the funny things he did, both on purpose and by accident. Watching "Cricket" run down a San Francisco street – chasing a taxi that still contained his bags – is a favorite, as is the time when he chased a basketball during an out-of-town practice and jumped over a railing that collapsed, sending his long legs sprawling out from under him. Warren helped lighten the mood during our yearlong quest.

One of the most important moments mentioned by the team is the meeting held in Jimmy Black's and Chris Brust's room toward the end of the season. Most team members feel that was the turning point. We decided we wouldn't "hurt the team" by foolish behavior. I was Jimmy's and Chris's suitemate, and still can vividly picture all the guys shoehorned in that tiny room. It was a special moment.

I believe that was when everyone on the team became focused on winning the national championship. That is when the idea of being national champions became more than words, more than an ultimate goal. It became reality.

The leadership of Jimmy Black also became more and more evident from that point on. He is the one player mentioned by the players, coaches, and staff as being the key to our team's success. Jimmy grabbed the reins and led us to the championship.

The championship ring was another thing that always came up during my conversations with team members. "Do you still wear yours?" "Where do you keep it?" "What do people say about it?"

One of the most touching stories involving the ring was Lynwood Robinson's. He had given it to his mother for all she had done for him. A few years later, a tornado destroyed their home, but the ring was found.

Members of our team have gone their separate ways, but we will always share the common bond of the championship. And we know now that is not just a trophy. It's a symbol of friendship, teamwork and achievement.

I still watch to see if Carolina players miss their layups. I see their manager watching, too. Often, I wonder if there really is any relationship between missing layups and winning ball games. We only lost two games that year, and we missed few layups.

I guess I would not have written this if we had lost to Georgetown. But even if we had lost, our team was still a unique group that shared many good times and emotions. The championship just seemed to strengthen those values.

It doesn't seem that 10 years have passed since that championship season. The decade has come between us. We don't all keep in touch anymore. My hope is that the words and photographs in this book helped to fill in some of the spaces and to rekindle fond memories for teammates and fans alike. ■

Acknowledgements

There are many people who need to be thanked for their help in getting this project out of my head and into print. Without their assistance and tireless efforts, *One To Remember* would not be.

A special thanks to Bob Inman, anchorman at WBTV News in Charlotte and author of the novels *Home Fires Burning* and *Old Dogs and Children*. His direction and advice in the early stages were the catalyst in getting this book going.

Bo Hussey, Director of Publications for the Charlotte Hornets, was a great help during the NBA season.

Thanks to Kay Thomas, UNC basketball secretary. Her support and advice were greatly appreciated. She is a good friend to the "Carolina Family."

Dane Huffman, of the Raleigh *News and Observer*, and David Rhew, of WBTV News, did an excellent job of proofreading and editing. Thanks also go to Dane for his help with interviews, titles, and information. His insight was a great help.

The sports information departments of Appalachian State, Kansas, Texas, UNC, UNC-Charlotte, and Vanderbilt gave of their time and efforts in helping me secure access, find old photographs, and gather statistics and other pertinent information.

Wish I Could of North Carolina has really opened my eyes to the good a small group of determined people can do. Jan and Darryl Hargett continue to enlighten less fortunate lives in our state, and I'm glad I have been able to help them in a very small way. They have definitely inspired me with their faith, honesty, and goodness.

Thanks to all the former players who graciously gave of their time for interviews. Tracking all of you down wasn't easy, but your thoughts and insights were well worth all the work.

John Kilgo's excellent introduction is an added bonus. I don't know where he finds the time to do all the things he does, but I'm glad he found the time for this great retrospective.

And thanks to Bob Leverone of the Charlotte Observer, Chuck Burton of the Associated Press, and Jim Morton for their excellent photography. Jim is Hugh's son, and filled in for him during the NBA All-Star Game in Charlotte in 1991. It was a game that Hugh wanted desperately to shoot, but a "flu bug" kept him at home on the mountain. Jim stepped into his dad's shoes and filled them admirably.

Hugh Morton. What can I say that hasn't already been said? Not only did he provide photographs from throughout the past decade, but he took some magnificent shots to update the Tar Heels' current lives and give true meaning to *One To Remember*. But he did not stop there. He was a continuous flow of support and encouragement. His phone calls and letters kept me going. He believed in me and supported me throughout. Thank you doesn't seem to be enough, but it will have to do.

And finally, thanks to my teammates, the coaches, and the staff of the 1982 North Carolina basketball team. I hope you had as much fun being a part of this book as I had putting it together. All your time, thoughts, insights, pictures, and quotes have truly made *One To Remember* a one-of-a-kind project. That makes sense because we are truly a one-of-a-kind team. GO HEELS! ■

Wish I Could
of North Carolina, Inc.

A portion of the royalties from *One To Remember* are being donated to Wish I Could of North Carolina, Inc.

Wish I Could is a non-profit, tax-exempt, all volunteer organization that grants wishes to any child between the ages of 1 and 18 who is suffering from a chronic or life threatening disease and is under the care of a North Carolina medical doctor.

Wish I Could works to bring special moments to children whose lives are filled with pain, fear, tears, and often the threat of death.

"We cannot give to them the gift of health, but we can give to each child their wish come true," says Jan Hargett, President of Wish I Could of North Carolina, Inc.

Wishes take many forms. Since its inception in 1987, Wish I Could has granted over 90 wishes to children across North Carolina. The types of wishes granted include meeting a celebrity such as Michael Jordan, receiving go-carts, computers, a new bedroom set and visiting Mickey Mouse at Disney World.

How can you make a wish happen? If you know of a child who would qualify, and would like to have more information, please contact:

Wish I Could of North Carolina, Inc.
P.O. Box 220563
Charlotte, North Carolina 28222
704 847-5661

Michael Jordan meets with Wish I Could recipient David Cornwell in the Chicago Bulls locker room. *Photo courtesy of Eastover Elementary School.*

120